How to Raise the Perfect Dog

HOW TO RAISE
the Perfect Dog

*Everything You Need to Know from
Puppyhood to Adolescence and Beyond*

Adam Spivey
of Southend Dog Training and

Evan Norfolk

RODALE

NEW YORK

First published in Great Britain in 2023 by Southend Dog Training Ltd.

Published in the United States by Rodale Books, an imprint of Random House, a division of Penguin Random House LLC, New York.
RodaleBooks.com | RandomHouseBooks.com

RODALE and the Plant colophon are registered trademarks of Penguin Random House LLC.

Library of Congress Cataloging-in-Publication Data
Names: Spivey, Adam, author. | Norfolk, Evan, author. Title: How to raise the perfect dog : everything you need to know from puppyhood to adolescence and beyond / Adam Spivey of Southend Dog Training and Evan Norfolk
Description: First edition. | New York : Rodale Books, [2023]
Identifiers: LCCN 2023027950 (print) | LCCN 2023027951 (ebook) | ISBN 9780593797099 (trade paperback) | ISBN 9780593797105 (ebook)
Subjects: LCSH: Dogs—Training. | Dogs—Behavior. | Puppies. | Pets.
Classification: LCC SF426 .S65 2023 (print) | LCC SF426 (ebook) | DDC 636.7—dc23/eng/20230613
LC record available at https://lccn.loc.gov/2023027950
LC ebook record available at https://lccn.loc.gov/2023027951

ISBN 978-0-593-79709-9
Ebook ISBN 978-0-593-79710-5

Printed in the United States of America

Book design by Andrea Lau
Cover photograph by Cristian Barnett

10 9 8 7 6 5 4 3 2 1

First U.S. Edition

CONTENTS

CHAPTER 4
Bringing Your Puppy Home 33

CHAPTER 5
Training Begins 46

CHAPTER 6

Putting Your Training into the Real World 72

CHAPTER 7

Common Mistakes and Practices 89

CHAPTER 8

Adolescence: A New Type of Terror!   99

CHAPTER 9

Frequently Asked Questions   107

Contents ix

INTRODUCTION

What's going on, guys? Adam here from Southend Dog Training. If you've got a puppy already or you're thinking about getting one in the future, there is tons of advice and guidance to help you with what is—let's be very clear—a pretty massive step in life. If you've seen any of my videos on TikTok or articles on my website, you'll know I'm all about keeping things simple and saying it like it is.

This no-bullsh*t approach takes all the nonsense out of dog training and puts your dog at the center of everything you do. You'll hear me say again and again that I like to train the dog that's in front of me, not follow a set of rules or guidelines that, it might turn out, don't even apply to your puppy, and that's what you'll find here. Because for me, the dog always comes first.

It will probably not surprise you when I say I love dogs. Everyone should have a dog, in my opinion: no home or family is complete without one. And when you bring a puppy into your life, you get to watch that puppy grow. They're with you through all the special occasions, the Christmases, the holidays, and the new babies. They become a part of your family, and when you lose them, it is absolutely crippling. Their loyalty and love are things that cannot be matched. And I'm proud to say that the dogs who've been a part of my family's life have been, and still are, my best friends—just like the saying goes.

However, I've learned that puppies—as with my kids—need to be prepared for and raised the right way. We don't just go to the hospital one day, have a baby, and expect them to fit into our world, or to know how to behave perfectly from the day they are born; we teach them and show them what it's all about, right? Whether that's about setting up a cot for them to sleep in, helping them to sleep through the night, teaching them how to ask for something nicely . . . or to not stick their fingers into electrical outlets. We praise and reward them when they get things right and let them know it's not OK when they do the wrong thing. Or at least that's how I raise my kids. It's hard work and requires attention, focus, and consistency. But the payoff down the line is a family I'm proud of and who I can always trust to do the right thing.

It's the same with my dogs. The first twelve months or so of a dog's life are, without a shadow of a doubt, the hardest work. Puppies are literally walking land sharks. Left to their own devices, puppies will p*ss and sh*t everywhere, eat all your furniture, use any available human being as a chew toy, and generally wreak havoc across every aspect of your life. Why wouldn't they? They're puppies! They have no idea how to behave in a human society. And you won't be surprised when I tell you that puppies who don't get the guidance they need through these vital, formative months grow into adult dogs who are just as chaotic and destructive. Only now they're massive and have really big teeth. Let me tell you this: dogs do not grow out of their bad behavior.

And, in fact, for a few months toward the end of their puppyhood, they actually start to behave even worse! Yes, folks, I'm talking about canine adolescence. In this period—just like us human beings when we become teenagers and cause all sorts of chaos—puppies can become rebellious and seem to be attracted to risk in a way they weren't before. It's important to persevere through this phase, and the only way to do that is to understand it. And yet so many people don't take the time to do this and end up taking their dogs to a rescue center or returning them to the breeder.

I blame the parents

It's basic common sense that you need to show a puppy how to do things right and let them know—without ever being cruel—when their behavior is wrong. Often, I meet people who tell me they haven't got the time to train their puppy; they're too busy or tired. Or worse, the people who think that all puppies need is love and cuddles and they'll somehow magically grow up into well-behaved dogs. Sorry, but this isn't Disney. That ain't going to happen and is actually being cruel. Puppies need guidance. I read about dog attack after dog attack in my local news, especially since the pandemic and lockdowns of 2020 and 2021. Too many people are getting puppies and then overlooking the fact that they are not toys but animals who need to be guided and supported through the very tough first year of their lives in the human world.

I say it again and again, having a puppy is hard work. Not

because of the puppy—they can't help being a puppy—but because of how much of YOUR time and effort is required to train them properly. You have to be strict and strong, patient and kind. You have to have boundaries and routines and stick to them, no matter how tired you are, what time of the night it is, or how much you just can't be bothered! You have to do all this to get the good-natured, well-behaved dog you are picturing in your imagination. So when you go online one rainy Sunday and start searching for that perfect dog, just bear this in mind—if you don't do all of these things, it will no longer be an achievable reality.

Hard lessons learned

You might think I've got some strong opinions about this stuff— and you'd be right! I have zero tolerance for anyone who isn't prepared to put in the time their dog deserves, especially when they are so young. If dog training inconveniences you, don't get a dog. And don't read this book. (There are quite a few other things I don't want to hear from people with dogs, like "It's OK, they're friendly," but more on this later.) My opinions come from experience, the result of which was very sad. I have been "that" dog owner who didn't do the research to understand what I was taking on, and it's a story that didn't end well. When I first decided to get a dog, I did what most people do when they want to buy anything these days; I went online. An hour or so later, I was off to pick up my new puppy—Jess—a little Staffordshire bull terrier. Happy days, right? How f**king wrong could I have been?

I remember noticing at the time that this guy's house was a bit of a sh*t heap, and when I asked him where the mom was he said she was in the other room because she could be a bit aggressive. Jess and her littermates were all locked up together in a cage and the whole thing was a bit of a dirty mess, if I'm honest. Still, I was so set on having her that I chose to ignore all of that—I just wanted to get her and get out of there, which I did. The guy didn't ask me where I lived, what kind of life she would have with me, or anything about who I was; he just took the cash and off we went.

Happy days, right?!? I know now that all the red flags were there. This guy was a backyard breeder who was only in it for the money. The welfare of his animals wasn't on his list of concerns. He didn't know or understand the art and science of dog breeding, he just wanted to make a quick buck. It was a recipe for tragedy, and one day, sure enough, Jess collapsed in the park. She died on the way to the vet shortly afterward. She was sadly just 16 weeks old.

With the benefit of hindsight and over ten years' experience training dogs from all walks of life, I can clearly see where I went wrong (we'll come to this and the best, most responsible way to find your puppy in chapter 1). I was devastated by losing her and vowed from then on to make sure I was better prepared and knew exactly what I was getting into. I did my research, read a pile of books on dog training, and soaked up pretty much everything I could about puppies and how to get it right. I was still too terrified to take on another puppy though, so I decided to look into giving a home to an adult dog who needed one.

We found Sammie—who's on the cover of this book—who was 16 months old and was being given up by her owner because she kept having fights with the other dogs in the house. The alarm bells were ringing loud and clear, ladies and gentlemen.

When I went to get her, it quickly became apparent that she was being denied some of her basic needs. As a dog with loads of energy, she needed (and still does) a lot of exercise—she was bouncing off the walls. When we left, she literally dragged me out of the house and didn't look back. I knew it was important that I spent time with her exercising before I took her anywhere near my house, so we went straight from there and walked for over two hours.

I wanted to get all that surplus energy out of her system and use the time together to establish what this relationship was going to be about. That walk has stayed with me ever since; it was kind of magical. It was raining buckets, but we were out for ages, just getting to know each other. I didn't want to go home with her until I felt sure she understood who was in charge (me), that she needed to listen to me and not be jumping up at people, pulling on the leash, ignoring me, or generally taking the p*ss. And that if she could do that, her new life would be sweet.

Daisy, my Rottweiler, was the next chapter in my dog life. Sadly, she is no longer with us as she passed away in December 2019 from cancer. But, boy, did she teach me a lot about puppy-hood! With Daisy, I did everything right. I got her from a decent breeder at the right time (she was almost nine weeks old). But still, I made a sh*t ton of mistakes! For one thing, I used puppy pads and had her p*ssing and sh*tting all over the house for weeks. And one time, she ate a Christmas tree, a box of Quality Street candy, and a CD all in one sitting. That dog really did have a bionic stomach!

At first, I thought I'd made a massive error of judgment and brought home the world's worst a*hole of a Rottweiler. But, in reality, it was me who was making all the mistakes. I was the a*hole. I wanted the perfect dog. One I could hug on the sofa and watch TV with. I realized quickly that I would need to put in some more work! You see, the dog I wanted wasn't something that just magically happens; you have to put the time in.

Realizing this changed everything. I put Daisy on a strict routine and began to understand her breed and what she needed to feel content. And I implemented nap time for her—yes, like a baby, your puppy needs regular naps and routine! To get what I wanted, I had to put my needs to one side and fulfill the dog's needs—more on this "breed fulfillment" later.

And I'll let you know that Daisy went on to help me help thousands of dogs all over the country. A dog, but not an a*hole dog.

Staffies and Rottweilers get a lot of bad press and there's a load of stigma around them being aggressive and dangerous and all that stuff, so I was hell-bent on making sure Sammie and Daisy were the best-behaved, well-trained dogs that ever lived. However, this wasn't for the benefit of other people and their opinions (I'm a big believer in not giving a f*ck about what other people think, and we'll talk about the expectations of other people and why it's your dog who comes first a bit more later on), but because I wanted a dog who wasn't an a*hole. I mean, I wanted a dog who would be a real part of our family's life, one who I could take on holiday and go on adventures with.

I worked nights at that time, so I'd finish work, come home, get the dogs, and head to the park, where we'd just spend hours going through different commands and building the relationships. I did a lot of off-leash heel work with them, things like getting them to lie down and stay until I called them—often from the other side of the park! It was pretty impressive to watch, to be fair. And most mornings we'd get a few spectators. I think because the sight of a dog and its owner working together so well is (a) kind of unusual these days and (b) pretty awesome. One morning, a man approached me with his Labradoodle, Alfie, and asked me if I would be interested in training him. I thought he was joking at first, but he reassured me he was serious and, without thinking about it, I said yes. When I got home later and told my wife, she said I had to do it because I'd said I would—we don't go back on our word in my family—and, to cut a long story very short, Southend Dog Training was born.

Honestly, I'd never even considered dog training to be a career; I didn't even know people made a living from it. I started doing training videos and posting them on social media and quickly realized that people liked the real-life, simplistic, no-bullsh*t way that I do things. If you've ever watched any of my training videos, you'll know I don't give a toss about what outfit I'm wearing when I'm doing an online tutorial (it's always my trainers and a hoodie anyway)—that's real life, folks. There are many egos in dog training with people who are more concerned about their own image than the dog in front of them. But more than that, too many trainers seem unprepared to tell their clients when they are getting it wrong or to hold them accountable for their dog's behavior. There's none of that with me and Southend Dog Training (SDT). I will not hesitate to tell you if I think you need to hear some hard truths. People are too worried about what other people think of them. And the irony is that it's exactly this lack of focus on the dog that leads to the bad behavior they are worried about in the first place. It's a dangerous feedback loop that no one or their dog needs to be caught in. Because when you stop caring about other people's opinions and focus on becoming your dog's biggest ally, that's when you really start making progress. Frikkin' anybody can do this!

The lockdowns of 2020 and 2021 saw a giant surge in dog ownership. According to the Dogs Trust in the UK, something like half a million extra dogs were acquired during this period. Half a million extra puppies, many of whom went to first-time owners, causing mayhem all over the country! It kind of blows your mind. With no in-person puppy classes to go to, and many of the usual opportunities for training and socializing just not available to people and their puppies, Southend Dog Training's online videos and resources quickly became a vital source of information and support for all the new dog owners out there. Not only because they are full of great advice and real-world situations, but because they are bite-size and relatable, and we don't overcomplicate things. Today, we have over three million followers on social media, and people view our online training videos from Southend to South Africa. With this book, I wanted to take all the lessons, information, and support that the global online Southend Dog Training community loves and put it together in one easy-to-use manual.

While I am not shy about my disdain for people who don't take the time to train their dogs, I do get that life is busy and people who don't work with dogs all day (like me) might need to take things in small steps. As a father of three, I know the importance of working smarter, not harder. That's why everything is broken down into simple instructions, with clear sections on everything you need to know about the first 12 months. From how to find the right puppy for you and those early days and weeks, through to what to feed them (we'll talk about RAW Southend Dog Nutrition later, people!), the tools you need (and the tools you really don't), and how to get out and about safely and securely, on and off the leash. We'll also look at the difficult period of adolescence and help you understand why the puppy you thought you were raising has suddenly become a major pain in the backside (it won't last, I promise you).

We'll get into the whole song and dance, but for now I just want to give you one piece of advice before you set off on this incredible journey, and it is this: *lower your expectations*. You're not going to have a perfect, well-behaved puppy from the word *go*. You're going to have a puppy that is excited, curious, and easily distracted by everyone and everything they come across. It's going to be hit-and-miss for a while, maybe more than a while. And that's OK. Puppies are babies. At this stage, the main thing

I want you to do is to focus on building confidence, yours and theirs. And on getting those basic life skills in place, like having them walk alongside you without pulling, and going to the toilet in a place that is not inside your house, respecting thresholds and having regular nap times.

It will be time-consuming and draining and sometimes you'll ask yourself why the hell you got this dog in the first place (I know, I have been there). But I urge you to make this investment in your puppy now because if you do, you get to sit back and enjoy the next decade or so of life with a well-trained, healthy, happy dog—your best friend—at your side.

Now, let's get this party started!

How to Raise the Perfect Dog

CHAPTER 1

Choosing the Right Dog for You

I firmly believe there is a dog out there for everyone, but to choose the right one, you need to be realistic about your limitations and what you can give them. Buying a puppy is almost as easy nowadays as ordering this book online. But the truth is, a puppy isn't a product you can stick in a cupboard and forget about if you don't like it. And they are definitely not something we should buy just because they'd look nice in our house . . . or because they're popular right now . . . or because someone down the road has just got one . . . or you've seen one you like on TV.

Have a word with yourself before you even start thinking about looking for a puppy. You have to be realistic about what you can bring to the table. You might think you're going to get fit by walking your dog every day—and this is true—but can you put your hand on your heart and say you'll be able to give a dog the exercise it needs for the next ten, maybe even fifteen, years? An under-exercised dog will undoubtedly make your life hell (you'll make their life hell too).

And what about training? Yes, this book will show you how

to train your dog. But it's not going to physically do it for you. That's still your job, I'm afraid. Training is time-consuming and requires your total focus and attention, especially in the early days when your puppy is learning so much and taking everything in like a mad thing. Then you've got to find the money to feed them, and vet bills can add up, especially if your dog's breed has specific problems. And then there's a thing called BREED FULFILLMENT.

What is breed fulfillment?

You'll want to know about this as I'll talk a lot about it in this book. As we know them today, dogs have come from a long line of ancestors who were bred for a specific purpose, from hunting and guarding to rescuing or just sitting on someone's lap (that's why they're called lapdogs).

Whatever your dog was originally bred to do is called its breed genetic disposition, the characteristics and instincts that have been bred into their physical and psychological profiles over centuries. Maybe your greyhound needs bursts of intense speed every day—that's their genetic disposition to race—or your terrier needs to pull and "rag" on toys to emulate how they might pull a rat out of a hole.

Fulfilling these basic genetic urges through the kind of play, activities, and general lifestyle you give your puppy is called breed fulfillment. It's about helping your dog behave in its most natural and instinctive way. And like all of us, dogs are happiest and at their best when their basic needs are being met. More on breed fulfillment as we go along, but here's a GOLDEN RULE: Ask yourself if you can deliver what's necessary to keep your dog stimulated and breed-fulfilled in the right way.

As well as breed fulfillment, there are a few other things I want you to think about and ask yourself or discuss with your family or partner—or basically anyone else who is going to be involved in the dog's life.

These are especially important if this is your first time owning a dog:

- **What size dog do you want?** Yes, size matters! Small dogs are generally cheaper to buy equipment for and take up less room on your sofa. Their food bills are smaller, and generally, their poos are too. They are also easier to transport and tend to live longer on average. Big dogs have a much larger presence; you will always know they are there. Larger dogs can generally handle a bit more rough-and-tumble.
- **Exercise requirements.** Every dog has different exercise needs, both physical and mental. Be realistic about how much time you can give that dog daily. Do not be fooled into thinking small dogs need less exercise! Dogs who have been bred for working (shepherds, spaniels, terriers, etc.) will require a lot of exercise and make your life difficult if they don't get it.
- **Are you passive or assertive?** This is an important one. If you are a passive owner, you might want to swerve from the headstrong breeds, such as bulldogs, as they will

exploit you given half the chance! Passive owners would be more suited to something with a soft nature, such as a greyhound.

- **How much does the dog shed?** If you are dreaming of a blue-eyed husky, are you also prepared to vacuum the carpet five times a day? You will have fur in your dinner, bath, and cup of tea! It's relentless. If you want a dog that doesn't shed tons, look at something like a Labradoodle or other so-called hypoallergenic breeds (but remember, there is no such thing as a fully hypoallergenic dog; it's all about their saliva and how much they slobber).

- **Slobber!** That's right; everyone loves a St. Bernard until they have slobber dripping from their ceiling! You must take this into consideration—larger dogs tend to be more slobbery. If you're the sort of person who keeps everything nice and tidy, this dog will not be your friend.

- **Health.** Breeding will play a part in this, but generally speaking, certain breeds have fewer ailments than others. Potential vet bills are definitely something to consider. Brachycephalic dogs (dogs with flat faces like pugs and French bulldogs) will often have more health issues than, say, Border collies, who tend to have very few health issues.

- **Breed fulfillment.** I know, I've said it already, but it is so important I'm saying it twice. Can you actually meet your dog's breed requirements—the impulses and drives that they have been bred for? Can you incorporate that, or something similar, into the training? An unfulfilled dog will be miserable and will make your life miserable too.

Now don't get me wrong, I'm not trying to put you off. I love dogs, and I think everyone can benefit from having one in their life. If you're still unsure which breed is right for you, let me suggest a few that I think make brilliant first dogs.

My top five first-time dogs

Every trainer and dog lover will tell you something different about what breeds are best for you. At the end of the day, it's your choice. But these are my top five dogs for a first-time owner. I've chosen them based on a decade's experience of working with breeds of all sorts and seeing firsthand some of the common problems among dogs. These five are all typically easygoing, good-natured, smart, and willing to learn. The Rottweiler man in me can observe occasional "over-friendliness" in these breeds, but that's not a bad thing for beginners, and basically makes them perfect for the novice trainer. If your heart is set on an American bully, but you've never had a dog before, think about having one of these dogs first—you can always grow your family later on (but, PLEASE, never get a second dog until your first one is properly trained!).

Golden retrievers

There's a reason these dogs are favorite dogs for families—they're calm and very affectionate (soppy). They are extremely intelligent and energetic, so they are easy to train and great for families who like the outdoors. They're classed as medium-sized dogs, but some of them can get pretty big. Grooming requirements are fairly minimal (barring some heavy shedding), just a decent brush twice a week is all you really need, along with the occasional nail trim.

Newfoundland

These gentle giants are originally from Canada, where they were bred to help humans with everything from sea rescues and hauling fishing nets to pulling logs and retrieving. They've got big, shaggy coats and, in my experience, slobber everywhere. But they're also fiercely loyal, loving, and intelligent, making them an excellent choice for first-time dog owners, especially families. They're not small though, so make sure you've got the room. They will grow up to be very strong dogs, so training from the get-go is essential.

Leonberger

As with the Newfoundland, this is a big dog with a big heart, with the bonus of looking kind of like a lion (they were originally bred in Germany to look like lions!). Confident but not aggressive, friendly but not crazy, these are great first-time dogs—but again, only for those with the space at home.

Labrador retriever

Labradors are the nation's favorite pet dog, and for good reason. They're clever, kind, affectionate, and calm. It's no coincidence they're the breed used as guide dogs for the blind—they are just so smart and reliable. You can't go wrong here.

Border terrier

Border terriers are small and short-haired, so they shed far less than dogs with longer coats. In my experience, they are a highly intelligent breed and generally very easy to train. They're also exceptional with people and children and have bags of character. They were originally bred to hunt rodents, so they're determined and brave—but getting socialization right is key to avoiding aggression toward other animals.

At the end of the day, whichever breed you choose, this book will help you. Just remember this GOLDEN RULE: YOU'VE GOT TO PUT THE WORK IN!

What about crossbreeds?

Of course, not all dogs are so-called purebreds, and there are plenty of crossbreeds around (although, if you want to get into it, you could argue that purebreds are also crossbreeds, but let's not split hairs!). I'm a big fan of mutts and my dog Roxy is a terrier crossbreed. The right crosses can make some of the best dogs and some combinations are now so popular that they are almost standalone breeds; I'm talking Lurchers (Border collie and grey-hound), cockapoos (cocker spaniel and poodle), and the like. The downside when considering crossbreeds is that you can't always know exactly what breeds or crossbreeds their parents were. This can sometimes mean you have more questions than answers re-garding some of the fundamentals on my checklist. It can also make breed fulfillment especially difficult. How will you fulfill the breed's genetics when you don't know what the breed is?

Do not fear. There is a thing called dog fulfillment. This is about meeting the needs of the dog in front of you, not neces-sarily the breed. For example, we know that things like scent and sound drive all dogs; they like food, and they are—at their core—predatory animals. So even if we don't know much about a dog's breed genetic disposition, we can incorporate our under-standing of their basic needs into our training to satisfy the dog. And, of course, we can observe and work with the dog in front of us. More on this soon.

CHAPTER 2

Finding a Breeder or Rescue Center

So, ladies and gentlemen, you've thought long and hard about the right dog for you, your family, and your lifestyle. And you've been brutally honest with yourself about your ability to meet the needs of the breed you chose. (I sincerely hope you have, anyway.) The next step is to go out and get one. The first question you're going to ask yourself is this: Where the f*ck do I start?

Dog breeding tends to be spectacularly unregulated. As a result, any Tom, Harry, or, excuse me, but total D*CK, can breed their dog and flog a puppy to the first puppy-struck idiot who comes along. Now, plenty of good-hearted people out there might have a litter of puppies—perhaps because they want to continue their own dog's line—and I don't have a problem with this kind of breeder. They're not usually in it for the money and just want the best for their dogs.

Unfortunately, plenty of less-well-meaning people exploit the lack of regulations and the gullibility of most people looking for a cute puppy to turn a quick buck. I'm talking about puppy farms and backyard breeders, people.

Beware of backyard breeders

The lockdowns of 2020 and 2021 saw a huge rise in the number of people taking on new puppies. We all had more time at home and, for many of us, getting a dog was the apparent answer to all of our problems of loneliness and isolation. But here's the thing people don't think about—the enormous spike in demand for puppies was fueled by thousands of unscrupulous breeders who were literally pumping puppies out of their exhausted and maltreated dogs to get the maximum amount of cash they could for the minimum amount of effort. These people have no regard for the health or welfare of the puppies they bring into the world.

It was particularly problematic for the so-called fashionable breeds—dogs like your French bulldogs, American bullies, and cockapoos—who can come with some pretty hefty health problems, even in the best of hands. And due to backyard breeders—people with no breeding knowledge—playing God with these puppies, we saw a lot of dogs being born with severe health and behavioral problems.

After paying thousands of dollars for a "designer" puppy, people quickly realized that they couldn't look after them and couldn't afford the frikkin' crazy vets' bills that came with them. According to the Royal Society for the Prevention of Cruelty to Animals (RSPCA), the number of French bulldogs being "returned" to rescue centers increased by a staggering 1,500% in the five years between 2015 and 2020. And those are the official numbers. There are also countless thousands of unwanted puppies who don't ever make it to a rescue center.

Demand for dogs also saw an increase in puppy imports and third-party sales; young dogs were transported overseas in large numbers in low-welfare conditions and then sold online by people posing as breeders. The number of licenses issued in the UK for the commercial import of dogs more than doubled in 2019–20, to over 12,000. That's 12,000 people importing very young puppies in big containers, sometimes with up to 150 of them in there all at once. Long journeys like this in substandard conditions are not good for young puppies—many of whom have been poorly bred and may already have health problems—before going through an incredibly stressful and traumatic experience like that. More unhealthy puppies, more people spending stupid amounts of money on dogs that don't stand a chance and fueling a wildly out-of-control breeding industry. I'm trying to say that the whole puppy breeding thing is a massive sh*t show, and you need to know what you are doing.

Get savvy—decent breeder or puppy dealer?

Why am I telling you all of this miserable stuff? You just want a cute puppy, right? What does it matter where it comes from as long as you treat it right when you get it home? Because I want you to get real and spot the red flags so it doesn't end in disaster. Because it's this simple: once you know what to look for, good and bad, you stand a much better chance of bringing home a healthy, happy puppy who will be with you for many years.

Follow this checklist to see if the breeder you are talking to is decent or a dealer:

- **If you've seen their ad online, does it look legit?** Are the pictures of a real home, or have you seen the same pictures on other websites? The same goes for the telephone number. Is the description written normally, or have they "optimized" it with current popular words so that Google will rank them at the top of the search results?

- **Is the breeder American Kennel Club registered?** Not all breeders who aren't AKC-registered are bad and not all AKC-registered breeders are good. But having that affiliation means they meet some basic welfare requirements that you will want to have in place.

- **Is the breeder happy to let you see the puppies with their mom?** They should be in a whelping box with their mom for the first eight weeks. Anyone who is cagey about the mother and/or has separated the puppies from her too early is not doing their job properly.

- **If you're looking at crossbreeds, are they a cross that has been thoughtfully and carefully matched?** Use your brain: the puppy of a massive, grunty bulldog and a dainty little Chihuahua is not going to get that far in life, is it? Just because you can, doesn't mean you should. If the breeder doesn't seem to know what they are doing, guess what . . . they probably don't.

- **Is their home a sh*thole?** I'm not being a snob here, I'm just saying trust your gut. If this person can't keep their own home from being a disgusting pit, what does that tell you about their approach to breeding puppies for sale? You get me?

- **Will they actually let you come to their home?** If they're asking you to meet them at a service station or some other weird place, they are likely to be a third-party salesperson employed by the puppy farm to shift "product" (aka puppies). Remember: you get your gas and McDonald's at the highway service station, not your puppy.

- **Are they asking you questions?** Anyone who gives a sh*t about their puppies will want to know a bit about you and where they are sending their dog to live for the rest of their life. If the breeder you're talking to isn't asking you some serious questions, they're not likely to have great standards when it comes to the welfare of their dogs.

- **Have they done all the paperwork and all the health stuff?** There is now something called the Puppy Contract that all decent breeders should be happy to provide you with. It's a legally binding contract that outlines all the basic health checks the puppy's parents have had (things like hip scoring, heart, DNA; it varies from breed to breed) and states that, if for any reason, the buyer (that's you) needs to return the puppy, you'll bring it back to the breeder—and not leave it in a garbage can somewhere.

- **All puppies should be microchipped** and have had at least one round of vaccinations before they are sold, and your contract should include evidence of all this.

- **Does the puppy seem healthy?** I know you're not a vet, but again, I urge you to use your common sense a bit. Is the puppy happy and playful, or does it seem a bit lethargic? Runny eyes, difficulty walking, and difficulty breathing are all signs of potential health problems. A decent breeder won't mind you getting a second opinion, so don't be afraid to bring someone along with you who might be able to tell you more or even suggest a consultation with a vet.

- **Are they happy to let you visit the puppy a couple of times before you take them home forever?** Someone restricting access or trying to get the animal out of the way unusually quickly should be ringing alarm bells for you.

The sh*tty bit

If you find yourself in a situation where you're not sure the breeder you're dealing with is legit, you need to walk away. Hard, right? I know, I really do. Every inch of you will want to save those puppies, or one of them anyway. But it's this simple, ladies and gentlemen: if you give these people money, you are perpetuating the whole nasty business. Walk away if alarm bells are ringing. Dodgy breeding thrives because it takes place under the radar, so the authorities need to know about it when something isn't right.

To the rescue!

People think dog rescue centers are only for adult dogs, but newsflash: there are plenty of puppies in rescue centers too. How do puppies end up in rescue centers when they are so young? There are loads of reasons. People discover their bitch is pregnant and can't cope with the reality of having puppies, or they get one from a breeder and very quickly realize they have made a giant error. In theory, a decent breeder will want you to return an unwanted puppy to them (and its mom), but dodgy breeders won't take puppies back, so they end up at the rescue centers. Rescuing a puppy isn't for everyone. With a rescue puppy, you don't always know what has happened to them before you come into their lives. You might not get to see their parents, or even know their parents' breed. It's a bit of a leap of faith that you need to be prepared to take in the knowledge that your puppy's backstory might never be that clear.

The upside

There are some pretty awesome benefits to having a rescue puppy. For one thing, they are usually far cheaper than a private sale, and you'll know they will benefit from proper health checks and vaccinations from a vet. Depending on how old they are, they may also have had some early training. And, of course, the main thing is you are helping a puppy who might never find a home, and with that often comes an incredible bond between the dog and its owner. Some of the greatest dogs I've worked with—including two of my own, Sammie and Roxy—have come from a rescue background, so don't discount it as an option before you've really explored it. Follow your local rescue center's social media pages or talk to the staff there about the kind of puppy you are looking for—they might have one for you.

Which puppy in the litter?

If you're picking a puppy from a breeder, you need to give some thought to which puppy you're going to choose. Which is best, a girl or a boy? The runt or the top dog?

It all depends on the kind of owner you will be and the type of energy you want your puppy to have. I always laugh when people tell me their puppy somehow chose them. A puppy runs over to them, jumps all over them, licks their face, and they decide that this puppy is their destiny—it's love at first sight! No! That's just the biggest, most headstrong and willful puppy in the litter. And if that's what they're like at eight weeks old, imagine what they're going to be like at eight months when they're smashing their way through the dog park! Or, at the other end of the spectrum, people feel sorry for the so-called runt and decide it's their job to help this puppy because they have a savior complex. But this puppy is more likely to be nervous and have anxiety problems later on. If you aren't prepared to manage a dog who lacks confidence and work with them to build it, you could find yourself with a problem pup further down the line.

If you are a first-time or inexperienced dog owner, ideally

you want the one in the middle: the calm and affable puppy who is energetic, but not crazy, curious, but not anxious. At the end of the day, it all depends on you and the kind of dog you want. You might like crazy, in which case, fill your boots! Which puppy you pick will be up to you and will be determined, to some extent, by which ones are available. But one thing you should try to avoid doing is bringing home two puppies from the same litter. And if you are dealing with a breeder who is happy to let you take two puppies from the same litter, you really need to question how competent this breeder is.

People think having siblings will be nice for the puppies, and they will play together and look after each other. Sorry, but no. As I have already mentioned, this is not a Disney film. Just because two dogs come from the same litter doesn't mean they will share some kind of magical sibling bond and enjoy each other's company for the next 15 years. Quite the opposite, in fact. Littermates form a pecking order from very early on, and when you bring two of them home together, that stays with them and can grow and become enhanced. What this means, in reality, is that one of your dogs will always dominate the other, a situation that, if not carefully managed, can lead to all sorts of trouble.

Littermate syndrome, aka sibling aggression, is very common when you take two pups from the same litter into the same household beyond the eight- to ten-week mark. Littermate syndrome isn't exclusive to the litter either; two puppies of the same age from different litters can also still develop littermate syndrome. This syndrome is why puppies very often fight with each other as they get older. They form a very close—and often codependent—bond with each other (anyone with their own sibling will probably relate to this!).

Fixing littermate syndrome means working with them individually, something puppies need, but it can be a massive chore as they panic whenever they are separated. For this very reason, a decent breeder will never sell you two dogs from the same litter. Although some people will tell you they have raised two puppies from the same litter and never experienced this, the truth is they have dodged a bullet. As a dog trainer of ten years, I've seen enough disastrous littermate relationships to know that they are the exception to the rule.

If you have your heart set on having two dogs of a similar age grow up together, I recommend bringing the second dog into your family when your existing dog is a minimum of ten to twelve months old. This means that training will be well established with your first dog and that strong sense of littermate rivalry will be dormant. At the same time, there will still be less than a year between them in age, so that they will have years ahead of them to run and play and have the time of their lives together.

Pink or blue?

For dogs, sex is very much a black-and-white situation. You have bitches (the girls) and you have dogs (the boys), and each sex has its own characteristics that are worth thinking about before you bring one home.

Without being too controversial, I actually prefer bitches. All my dogs are bitches—mainly because when you give them a belly rub, you don't accidentally rub a penis. But also because, in my experience, females are more nurturing and loving and generally the kind of dog I like to have around the place. But, as with all species, when they kick off they really mean it! Males can be a bit goofier and emotionally detached. When they kick off, it's all bravado and "look at me, I'm Billy Big Bollocks." To make things more complicated, your breed will also play a part in gender charactcristics, so be sure to talk to your breeder or do some research about the breed you've chosen and how bitches and dogs can differ. You also need to remember that bitches have seasons during which they bleed and attract the attention of male dogs. And dogs like to mark their territory by p*ssing everywhere. When they pee, it's up something, whereas with bitches, it's usually on a flat surface.

It's a messy business, having a dog. You just have to choose which mess you want to live with for the next ten to fifteen years.

> **TIP:** *If you can't decide which puppy in the litter is right for you, but you know you'd like a bitch or a male, ask the breeder to briefly remove all of the puppies who aren't the gender you are after. This way, you aren't overwhelmed with puppies and can see the boys or the girls with fewer distractions.*

CHAPTER 3

Preparing for Your Pup

I once bought my two-year-old daughter a pair of eye-wateringly expensive Ugg boots, only for her to grow out of them in a couple of weeks. It's the same with puppies. They grow crazy fast! There are literally thousands of things you can spend your money on when it comes to a new puppy. I can't stop you from buying them a bow tie or a bed in the shape of a car, but let's be very clear: all that stuff is funny, but pointless. You don't need to spend a fortune on things that are not necessary at this stage. Think of your puppy as a blank canvas on which you are about to paint a masterpiece—you don't want to throw all of your brushes and every color paint at it all at once, do you? Too much too soon will leave you without any materials and a big old mess on the canvas.

In this chapter, I'm going to help you prepare for your new puppy; we'll look at all the tools you need to buy and all the stuff you really don't. I will also talk about their food and why I'm a big believer in a raw diet and hand-feeding. But before we go into all that, I want to mention one thing you need to keep in mind when preparing for your new arrival: A SMOOTH TRANSITION.

What do I mean? Well, if you think about it for a minute, you're basically taking this puppy away from everything it has known in its short life and transferring it to an entirely new human environment. The young dog, now essentially your child, doesn't care if it's got a nice bowl with its name on it or a dia-manté collar. They care about staying alive, food and protection, growing, using all their new skills, and satisfying their curiosity. Back in the litter with their mom and all their littermates, there were plenty of opportunities for play and stimulation, endless food and warmth. So when I say make it a smooth transition, what I mean is make sure, as far as you can, that all of these things are in place at your puppy's new home. Diamanté collars can wait.

One major NO

In a second, I'm going to give you my breakdown of all the things you'll need and why, but first, I want to tell you the one thing you definitely don't need to buy: PUPPY PADS. It doesn't matter how you dress them up, how the theory works, or how worried you are about your carpets getting ruined—puppy pads send a message to your dog that it's OK to p*ss and sh*t in your house. They encourage the EXACT OPPOSITE of the behavior you want your dog to learn. You are setting them up to fail, ladies and gentlemen; that is not what we are all about.

We'll come to toilet training properly in chapter 4, but for now, just remember this: puppy pads tell your puppy it's OK to sh*t and p*ss in your house. If you are OK with that, by all means, go out and buy a load of them. But if you want to teach your puppy to do their business outside, save yourself a load of hassle and cash and leave the puppy pads at the pet shop.

My list of pre-puppy essentials

Having a few essential bits of gear at home when you bring your puppy back for the first time will help you make that smooth transition that we all want. Here are my suggested essentials:

- **PUPPY CRATE (X 2)**

People get in a right old state about puppy crates and say they're cruel and you shouldn't keep a dog locked in a crate and all that nonsense. But ask yourself this: Would you put your newborn baby to sleep on the floor in the middle of the room or on a chair? No, you wouldn't. You'd put them somewhere safe, reassuring, and comfortable. That's all a crate is, a reassuring space for your puppy where they can rest and you can be sure they're OK.

Think of it as a den-like environment, similar to the whelping box they will have spent their first eight weeks in. They like it. We'll come to how to use a crate and crate training in the next chapter, but for now just make sure you've got one—and if you live in a house with stairs, preferably two (one for upstairs and one for downstairs).

You can get all sorts of crates with plastic windows and curtains—that's your choice at the end of the day. Just make sure you can open and close it easily and that your puppy can get in and out of the crate. A plastic base that you can easily clean will also be a bonus.

- **A TREAT POUCH FOR RAW FOOD**

Puppies frikkin' love food, and they love to chew sh*t! We'll be using food a lot over the next few weeks and months to build the bond between you and create motivation for your puppy. At Southend Dog Training, we're all about feeding our dogs raw food—yes, RAW. Why? Because it's a species-appropriate diet. It's not full of crap and it's great for their teeth and gums.

There's more about diet on page 26, but in the meantime, find yourself a treat pouch that is (a) easy to attach to a belt or keep in a pocket, (b) designed for easy access (on your belt or around your waist is perfect), and (c) hygienic. Silicone pouches are my preferred choice as you can easily wash and wipe them clean. If you worry about handling raw food, you might also want to invest in a load of latex gloves and hand sanitizer.

- **A PUPPY PEN**

This is not their crate for rest and switching off, it's a safe area for your puppy to play in at home. You can get a full pen or use gates to section off an area of your home where your pup can move around freely; just make sure it's safe and not full of dangerous chemicals or exposed wiring. You also need to be able to get in and out of the area easily, so don't put high boundaries there that make it difficult for you to move freely.

- ### A PUPPY COLLAR AND ID TAG

When getting your puppy's ID tag made, I'd suggest you put your name and address, your dog's name, and your telephone number on it. Also check your local laws about dog ID tags. At this stage, a collar needs to be soft and easy to take on and off, with room for at least two fingers between your puppy's neck and the collar. We'll come to getting them used to it in the next chapter; just make sure you have something at home ready for them to put on as soon as they arrive.

- ### INDOOR PUPPY TRAINING LEASH

This is essential; it will go on your puppy's collar every time they are out of the crate for the first few months. Go for a soft, long indoor training line—it should be thin and lightweight, almost ribbon-like. And with no handle at the end, as this prevents it from getting caught on things and risking strangulation.

- ### TOYS

You don't need to overwhelm your puppy with a sh*t ton of toys that they can access whenever they want to. When you let them get at toys whenever they like, you devalue the toys and your own leverage for training. We'll cover toys and how to use them shortly. In the meantime, pick up these few essentials at the pet shop (or from the SDT website, where everything is tried and tested by us) so you're game-ready when your puppy comes home:

- A tug toy or bite wedge: heavy-duty rope or something similar (not for the puppy to play with alone)
- A flirt pole: for using up some of that excessive energy
- A ball: for throwing and retrieving (not for the puppy to play with alone)
- An interactive food-dispensing toy like a LickiMat or KONG Classic: great for when you need to keep them busy without your supervision
- Something to chew on, like a nylon bone: for teething
- A brush for grooming

You need to get your dog used to being brushed, not so it looks nice and pretty, but so that their coat stays clean and so that they are comfortable with being handled by you, the groomer, or the vet. You can introduce a nice relaxing brush of their coat almost from day one, so make sure you have a brush at home. Different breeds and coats will need different brushes, but mostly with puppies you want something soft that isn't going to hurt their delicate skin.

Your puppy's diet

As with everything to do with puppy training, when it comes to their diet, you get out what you put in. It's that simple. I advocate a raw food diet from day one (yes, puppies can eat raw from the start, so don't fall for all that special puppy food bullsh*t at the supermarket), and I prefer to feed my dogs by hand. Raw food? By hand? YES! Here's why:

Hand-feeding

A massive part of the way I train dogs is based on hand-feeding, rather than bowl feeding, until they are fully trained. Hand-feeding is kind of like breastfeeding a baby. It's the best thing for them, but you don't want to do it forever! Hand-feeding your dog is the best and quickest way to build a bond between the two of you.

With every bit of food that passes from your hand to their mouth, you are strengthening the relationship between you and your dog. Not only that, but hand-feeding requires your dog to do something in return for their food. When you put their food in a bowl on the floor and walk away, you miss out on endless training and teaching opportunities. Your bowl-fed dog learns that its next meal is coming in a few hours, so the power of food as a motivator for training and good behavior is reduced.

If you're hand-feeding your dog, you're never really giving them "treats" or a "meal"—you're just giving them their food slowly throughout the day. You might be out on a walk, in the garden, or in the toilet—it doesn't matter where you feed them or at what time. If you are hand-feeding them, it happens throughout the day. So try to let go of the idea of set mealtimes and matching bowls.

But how do you know how much to give them? It's simple, guys. Work out your puppy's daily allowance of food according to its weight. Your food supplier should provide this information. If you don't have scales at home, you should be able to easily weigh your puppy at the vet—most vets have a scale in their waiting room. Put that food in your treat pouch and use it as the "treats" you reward your puppy with as you train them throughout the day.

> **TIP:** You can start this technique as soon as your puppy comes home, so make sure you have worked out their daily allowance before they come blasting through that door and smashing into their food.

Raw food

I like to feed my dogs a raw food diet. This doesn't mean going down to the butchers daily and buying them a load of steak. The raw dog food I recommend is Southend Dog Nutrition, which is nutritionally complete. It contains all the bones, organs, and meat your dog needs for a healthy, genetically appropriate diet. I'm talking beef trachea, spleen, tripe, chicken necks, lamb kidneys, and the works. It will also contain certain vegetables and berries, fish oils, and kelp. With a decent complete raw food, all these things will have been put through a grinder in the appropriate ratios, so you know your dog is getting the right amount of everything they need.

Why do I prefer raw? Just take a look at your dog's jaw! It's designed to eat this stuff. Plus, it's not full of preservatives and colorings that can cause allergies and digestive problems. And I've seen firsthand how much a raw food diet improves everything, from a glossier coat and stronger teeth (dogs fed on a raw diet do not need ridiculous dental sticks and toothbrushes—fact) and a better temperament—an all-around happier dog.

Benefits of a raw food diet

- Dogs drink less water: easier toilet training
- They don't fart as much (the dog, not you!)
- Feces are much smaller: literally less sh*t in their body
- Better teeth
- Improved temperament
- Less prone to allergies
- A stronger immune system

What's not to love? "But what about salmonella?" People ask me this a lot. Yes, full disclosure: your dog could get salmonella if they eat raw food. But hello—it's a tiny risk! In ten years of working with dogs, I've yet to come across a canine case of salmonella. It's the same as how they might choke on a bone. So could you. Choking is a risk—minimizing it is all about making the right choices and supervision. It's a risk, but it's not a risk that outweighs the benefits of a raw food diet.

Where do you get raw food? There are hundreds of brands making decent raw food for dogs now. You can go online and get it delivered to your door in the right size portions for your dog, or you can buy it from your local pet shop in slabs, which you can keep in the freezer and divide into the portions you need throughout the day. We, of course, 100 percent recommend our brand, Raw Food: Southend Dog Nutrition, which can be purchased from our website.

However you choose to do it, here are the key things you need to remember:

- You can feed a puppy raw food as soon as you bring them home.
- Follow your supplier's guide on how much to give them.
- Go for a complete raw food: this means it contains everything your puppy needs to grow.
- Always practice good hygiene: wash your hands and wipe surfaces.

But raw food and hand-feeding? Many people get a bit squeamish about this. They don't like the idea of handling squishy raw meat. It doesn't bother me, but I get it. There are two ways around this. One is to wear latex gloves every time you are feeding your dog. I know plenty of people who do this, but it's a bit of a pain in the arse having to put rubber gloves on every time you want your dog to do something.

The other option is to put your raw food into an old squeezy ketchup bottle or something similar and dispense it from the bottle directly into your puppy's mouth.

If you choose not to feed raw, that's OK! There are some decent dry foods and kibbles out there. But there are plenty of sh*t ones as well. Here are the things to look out for in decent dry dog food:

- It must contain proper meat, not a meat derivative: meat derivative is garbage.
- The meat should be the very first ingredient on the list: if it comes halfway down, after colorings and preservatives, it might as well just be dust.
- It should not be multicolored or shaped like something weird: the more messed around with their food is, the less natural it is.

Don't forget the water

Being a puppy is thirsty work. After a busy training session, ensure your pup has access to clean, fresh water. To help with toilet training, it's best not to give them totally free access to water just yet. Like us, dogs need to stay hydrated to keep everything working. Some dogs are messier drinkers than others . . . keep a towel nearby.

TIP: *Water is a big indicator of how healthy they are. If your pup is drinking excessive amounts of water, it could mean their food is not agreeing with them or they have an underlying illness. Keep an eye on things, and if in doubt, talk to your vet.*

Their name

It seems obvious, guys, but try to decide on a name before you bring them home, please! It's literally the first thing you're going to teach them and how you're going to help them understand that they need to pay attention to you when you say something to them. So have something ready . . . now is not the time to try out names and see if stuff suits them or anything like that.

You can call your puppy whatever you want, but some things will make your life easier than others. The main thing is to give them a name that's not easily confused with a command. You're going to be saying words like SIT, DOWN, and YES, so it might be a good idea to avoid Spit, Clown, and Ness. And if you've got a big menacing dog (for example, an American bully or a cane corso), please don't give them a big menacing name, like Brutus or Killer. It might be funny, but these aggressive labels only add to the misunderstanding around powerful breeds. It's no coincidence my Rottweiler was called Daisy. Keep it positive, people.

Patience

Stock up on this. Without it, you'll not get very far with this dog training game. What do I mean by patience? I mean, you can't get frustrated and lose your sh*t every time they have an accident on the kitchen floor or they don't stay put when you tell them to. You can't get frustrated with your dog for not understanding or knowing what they are meant to do. You are teaching them. If they get something wrong or don't seem to understand, that's your fault and not theirs. Stay calm and patient and you will get there.

Consistency

Repetition is key in training dogs. You do stuff with them, and you repeat it until they get it. They like rules and knowing where they are with things, so you need to be consistent. You can't decide they're not allowed on the sofa and then change your mind one evening because you want a cuddle. And you have to be consistent with the positive stuff too. That means always rewarding them—with a treat, a belly rub, or whatever it is—when they do the right thing. We'll go into more detail soon, but for now, just remember your consistency is what will help them learn. Told you it was hard work, didn't I?

CHAPTER 4

Bringing Your Puppy Home

OK, guys! So you've got the puppy, all the gear . . . and no idea, right? Don't worry! I'm here to talk you through the first few days of living with your new puppy. Not to freak you out or anything, but this is a REALLY important moment and getting it right now will help you stay on track further down the line.

The smooth transition I mentioned in the last chapter is a key thing to remember. Your little puppy's world has just been turned upside down. They will be relying on you to show them what to do now, so make sure you can give them loads of attention and generally be there for them in this transitional period. It's no good getting a puppy in the morning and then going off to work for the day. If you can't give them the time and focus they deserve right now, it isn't the right time for you to get a dog.

Bringing your puppy home for the first time

You can do a few things for your puppy to make that all-important transition to their new home go as smoothly as possible. This list is a guide—you don't need to rigidly do things in this order—but try to incorporate these key points into their first day at home with you.

Keep calm and carry on

When you bring your puppy through your front door, the first thing I want you to do is to make sure it's nice and quiet. Do not invite everyone you know over to meet your new puppy! All of that can wait. This is a baby animal experiencing major sensory overload. They've probably just been in a car for the first time and they might have traveled a long distance. They don't know what the frik is going on! Use your common sense here and give your puppy a calm and soothing first day or so in their new home.

That said, it's important to be realistic about the noise levels in your home from the get-go. If you have a busy family life, your puppy will need to learn to switch off while it's all going on around them. More on this coming up in the "Sleep" subsection.

Collar and leash

Now the first thing I want you to do is to put their new collar and leash on. You don't want to let your puppy just run all around the house. Firstly, the world is a big toilet to them right now, and if left to their own devices, they can—and will—p*ss and sh*t everywhere. But secondly, too much space will terrify the little guy or girl. A major mistake people make is letting their puppy explore too much, too soon. Putting their leash on lets them know they should stay close to you for now. There is loads of time for discovering the rest of the house later on. For now, just take your puppy into the rooms it is going to be allowed in. For most of us, that usually means the kitchen and maybe the living room. Have your pen set up in one of these rooms as a space they can roam freely in, then introduce them to that and let them discover things at a nice gentle pace.

> **TIP:** *Kids' bedrooms and puppies do not go well together. Unless you have the world's tidiest child or teenager, their room is likely to be full of toys, clothes, books, hairbands, and pretty much everything a puppy likes to chew—and potentially choke—on. I advise keeping certain rooms categorically off-limits to a puppy, kids' rooms being at the top of the list.*

Toilet training

We're not doing puppy pads, guys! So they need to learn to go outside for a number one or two. Obviously, this will take a while and there will be a few accidents along the way. But you can start introducing them to the idea that p*ss and sh*t stay outside from the moment you come home. Keeping them on the leash, take them outside and wait until you see them doing their business. Give them a treat, make a fuss, and add a command. For my dogs, it's always "Go toilet." This isn't going to happen overnight, but there is no reason why you can't start introducing the idea now. Most dogs want to go outside for this stuff; they're programmed to do it outside. So you have nature on your side, at least.

> **TIP:** *If your puppy is from a breeder and you're collecting them at the recommended eight weeks of age, they will not have had all their vaccinations yet. This means that the risk of picking up an infection from the ground (such as parvovirus) is increased. So you need to be extra careful about ensuring they stay safe until they have had that second round of vaccinations.*
>
> *Keep some dog-friendly, antibacterial animal wipes by the door or in your pocket and wipe your puppy's feet and belly when they come inside. This will ensure they stay safe until they get their next shots. If you live in an apartment, do the same thing in the communal gardens or nearby park.*

I am 100 percent opposed to using puppy pads, as it sends a confusing message to your pup. If you think it might be difficult to get outside in time (and often late at night), then you really need to consider whether having a puppy is right for you.

Tell them their name

Your puppy needs to know their name, right? Teaching them this is simple. Say their name and give them a treat. Say their name and give them a treat. Say their name and give them a treat—you get the idea. Do this for five or ten minutes, until you feel like they understand that something tasty comes their way when you say their name. They'll make a positive association between their name and you. Job done. (More on names and reinforcing positive associations in the next chapter.)

Introducing them to other animals

If you've already got a dog in the house, you must keep both dogs on a leash when they first meet. Take introductions slowly but do it almost immediately after you've taken them outside to go to the toilet. There are plenty of variables to consider here—every adult dog and puppy is different. Your puppy is a baby who might think your existing dog is a big chew toy. Some adult dogs are instinctively nurturing; others might get grumpy with a puppy bouncing all over them from the get-go. Take it slowly, praise calm behavior in your adult dog, and give them plenty of individual attention. They are different animals with different requirements. Your adult dog might have sofa privileges and not sleep in a crate, but that doesn't mean your puppy follows suit.

Introducing them to their crate

After all the excitement of coming home and exploring their new environment, it's important your puppy gets the rest they need. Once you've taken them outside for a pee and done their first little training session by teaching them their name, I want you to put them in their crate, close the door, put a blanket over it, and leave them to rest for a while. If the puppy starts to cry, you need to ignore it. Whining is part of the process; it is going to happen. It's not easy to hear, I know, but if you respond to it, you are making a rod for your own back. You are not being cruel; you are teaching them how to switch off and giving them a breather from all the stimulation of the day. The length of sleep will vary according to your dog's size and breed, but they should normally sleep for an hour or two at this stage and will need up to 16 hours of sleep a day. If they have only slept for a few minutes and start crying again, it hasn't been long enough. Ignore it and let them settle themselves back to sleep. This is tough love, guys, but it is worth it.

Introducing eye contact

Engagement. Eye contact. Paying attention. However you want to describe it, every single thing you teach your dog starts from this point. Without a dog who pays attention to you when you need them to, you won't be able to teach them anything! You can start teaching your puppy that good things happen when they pay attention to you from the get-go. It's a simple technique that

I call Just Say Yes. And as you might have guessed, it involves just saying "YES," then rewarding them with a treat when your puppy looks at you. The more you can reward eye contact, the more results you will get. It's a bit more involved than this (we'll look at YES and other markers more closely in chapter 5), but there is no reason why you can't start now with this simple technique.

Sleep, go toilet, play, and train: you can follow this kind of pattern as soon as you come home. Obviously, it's very early days and you don't want to overwhelm your puppy with training and commands on day one! But by following these steps as soon as you get home, you can begin to introduce them to some fundamentals and start to establish the bond between you.

Introducing your puppy to children

It's important to understand that children are towering giant strangers to your puppy. Don't let kids surround them or overcrowd them. Make sure the kids are sitting somewhere safe when they first meet the puppy, and explain that they'll need to be patient while the puppy finds its feet—or paws!

The puppy routine

The first few days will be a bit of a mental blur, let's face it. But pretty soon you should be able to establish a routine for your puppy. A routine, you say? But why does a dog need a routine? It's not a human being, right? Many people think dogs don't need routines and you should just let them do things on their own schedules. There is an argument for less restrictive routines, I believe, with older dogs, especially if you are the kind of owner who doesn't have a routine yourself. For example, you might travel a lot and need to leave your dog with other people for periods, or you might work unpredictable hours. It makes sense that a dog locked into a regular routine will find it stressful when things keep changing all the time. But for puppies, a daily routine is reassuring and helps them settle into their new surroundings.

Young dogs like to know where they are with things. It is also a massive win when it comes to toilet training. Putting that structure into their daily schedule means you'll know when they eat, when they sleep, and when they're likely to need to go to the toilet. Happy days! It's also about helping this young animal adjust to life in the human world.

Your life is busy, I know, so you need those windows of time when you know your puppy will be asleep or playing independently. A decent routine will create this space for you and your puppy. And the more support you can give your puppy through a reliable, consistent schedule, the better chance you're giving them of becoming a well-adjusted, happy adult dog.

So let's get you and your puppy set up with a routine! This is the schedule I have followed with all of my dogs, and it's the one I get all of my clients and students to live by. . . .

First thing in the morning, your puppy will have a full bladder and need a pee, if not a poo. Take your pup outside for the toilet, and when they go, praise them and start adding a "Go toilet" command. Remember, if they haven't had all of their vaccinations, you need to wipe them down when they come back inside.

Once your pup has been to the toilet, grab your pup's food and begin a training/play session: sit, down, eye contact, and reward, etc. (While you are waiting for them to be fully vaccinated, this can be any of the training ideas and techniques listed in chapter 5. Later on, when you can get out and about, there are more things you can do at the park, beach, or wherever you are.)

Once your pup starts mouthing things or losing interest in what you're doing, it's a sign they're overtired. We want to ensure your session ends positively, so give them a chew toy to calm them down, decompress, and help with any teething, then put them in their crate and let them sleep.

As soon as your puppy wakes up (roughly one to two hours), take them outside for a toilet break, followed by a training/play session until they seem tired. Repeat the above every time your puppy wakes up (on the basis they have had a good sleep for one hour or more).

Bedtime

It's important to let your puppy know there is a difference between night and day—and that you will not be available for fun and games after a certain time. Establishing a routine around bedtime will be reassuring and comforting for your puppy in exactly the same way as your daytime routine is. Once they've learned the basics and have grown up a bit, you can afford to switch things up. But in these early days, you'll need to call on all your consistency and patience while establishing a routine. I'm not going to dress this up: it's going to be hard. You're going to feel exhausted. But puppies are baby dogs, people. You're going to have some sleepless nights.

Just remember, it's only for a short while and you'll be rewarded with a puppy who sleeps through the night and doesn't p*ss on their bed.

Puppy bedtime routine and key points

- Don't feed your pup any later than 8 pm.
- Take your pup out for a pee, make sure they go to the toilet, do a training/play session, and put the pup back in the crate.
- About an hour later, take your pup back out for a pee and make sure they go to the toilet again and put the pup back in the crate.
- Just before you go to bed, take the pup out again for a pee, make sure they go to the toilet, and then put the pup back in the crate for bed.
- Your pup may cry for the first few days. You have to ignore this and let them cry it out. Do not get your pup out of their crate while they are crying—the moment you do this, you are teaching them that whining will get them let out.
- Set your alarm so you wake up every two hours during the night to let your pup out for the toilet. It is not fair to

leave them to have an accident because you want a straight eight hours of sleep.

Dogs are naturally hygienic, and it will be distressing for your puppy to spend a night in their own pee. If you notice that your dog is not going every two hours, set your alarm every two and a half to three hours and so forth, until you find the right stretch of time.

By the end of the week, you will have established a nice routine and can begin to push the length of time between pee breaks as your puppy learns to wait until you come to let them out.

If you live in an apartment: sorry, folks, but you still need to take them outside!

> **TIP:** *Get yourself some earplugs so you can more easily ignore any whining. If they have had a pee and they are safe in their crate, you don't need to worry about them— they are OK!*

A word about puppy biting . . .

Puppy biting is probably the top issue we are asked about when it comes to your cute little pup. Puppies are the definition of a walking land shark! As a rule, anything that touches them will go into their mouth, and generally anything they can put their mouth on they will. Now, we must understand that puppy biting is a completely normal behavior. It is their teething phase. We don't punish puppies for this; we manage it in a way that is beneficial for both the pup and ourselves.

Puppies will bite most when they first wake up and are full of beans, when they are overstimulated, and when they are overtired or frustrated. With this in mind, we want to be one step ahead, so as soon as the pup wakes up, we attach them to a puppy leash, we take the pup into the garden, we wait for them to go to the toilet, we praise this heavily, then we go into a training session. The use of food and/or a small tug toy for these training sessions will help the puppy. We are channeling the energy of the little land shark into something productive.

After this vigorous training session, we want to give them something to help them calm down and decompress. This is where the use of a chew, bone, or KONG comes into play. Not only will this provide some mental enrichment for the puppy and help calm them down, it will ease the teething and give them something productive to bite on.

After this it is nap time. If the puppy starts to bite you during training sessions or when it first comes out of the crate, this is what the leash is for—you can use the leash to easily hold the dog away from you, lead them to where you want them, or redirect them to chew on something more productive.

Don't squeal like a piggy

You may have heard that making high-pitched noises will deter puppy biting. Although in rare cases this could work, nine times out of ten it is only going to excite the pup more. Think about a squeaky toy: observe your pup's reaction when they hear the squeak and see how it excites them. This is the same when a puppy is biting you; a squeal can have an adverse effect.

Puppy biting does get easier provided you are consistent. It is unrealistic to expect the pup to never put its mouth on you. Remaining calm will help, and I promise you it gets better in time.

CHAPTER 5

Training Begins

So, guys, how are we doing? Ready to start properly training your new puppy? Hopefully, by now, you've already started cracking on with a few of the important things: you've given them a non-stupid name, you've brought them home and maybe even begun to take them outside for a pee, and they're getting used to their crate and their new surroundings. Awesome work! Now, until your puppy is ten weeks old, you can't take them out and about in the world. This is to help prevent the spread of a few nasty viruses that can really do a lot of damage to a puppy if they catch them. Puppies are vulnerable and they need their vaccinations, people! So make sure you have been to the vet and done all the necessary stuff to ensure they stay fit and well in these early weeks and months.

CHIP TIP: *Consider getting your puppy microchipped as early as eight weeks old. It means if your dog ever gets lost, it can easily be returned to you. Your breeder or rescue center may have microchipped the puppy before they come to you. You need to get the paperwork, guys! Make sure you have the documents and keep them safe, and if your puppy hasn't been chipped, get it done ASAP.*

If you are anything like me, you'll want to get out and about and have adventures with your puppy from the get-go. It can be frustrating to have to keep them at home for a little while. But this early incubation period at home is a wicked opportunity to focus on training the basics and building the bond and communication you will need with your pup.

Let's just have a quick recap over what you need to have in hand to make training go smoothly:

- Treat pouch: ideally attached to your belt and with easy access
- Their daily food allowance: ideally raw or good-quality dry
- Latex gloves or a squeezy ketchup bottle if you are using them
- Loads of patience and consistency
- Poo bags for outside and dog-friendly wipes

Before we start with specific commands and behaviors, I want to talk about what I think of as the real essence of the way

I train dogs: the Art of Attention and the Art of Doing Nothing. These two fundamental concepts form the basis of everything I am teaching you. They aren't specific commands but more a way of life that comes into everything you do with your pup. Let me explain . . .

The Art of Attention

Trying to teach your dog anything without first getting their attention, and secondly keeping it, is next to impossible. You want your puppy to learn that anything fun or exciting they receive comes, first and foremost, because they acknowledge you. When they learn that paying attention to you—usually with direct eye contact—leads to all the good things in life that they like, such as food and fun and fuss, you become the best thing since sliced bread, or dried turkey necks anyway!

For example, if you ask your puppy to sit before going for a walk, you have asked them to pay attention to you—they do it, so you go for a walk. Your puppy has learned that paying attention to you (looking at you and eye contact) and doing what you have asked them has enabled the walk to start. They begin to realize you're kind of important. It's why when you watch dogs competing at high levels, they all have their eyes fixed on their owners as they go around the course or do whatever is being asked of them. Attention is the foundation of all the behaviors you are trying to teach your dog here.

In a moment, we'll learn about how to get that attention and the different ways you can reward and motivate your puppy to consistently pay attention to you. For now, I just want you to keep the Art of Attention in mind as you progress through each paragraph and notice how it comes into everything I teach.

The Art of Doing Nothing

This might sound self-explanatory, but it's more complex and important than it sounds. We all need to switch off sometimes and puppies are no different. But because you are literally their whole world right now, it's sometimes hard for puppies to feel secure enough to know that it's OK to do nothing for a bit and that you will still be there when that rest time is over. Some dogs are naturals at switching off, and others need to be shown how to relax.

You will already have been practicing this by using their crate and putting them in there at the end of their training and play sessions. You will also have been teaching them the DOWN stay, and using your GOOD marker to increase the duration of that stay (this is explained later). But the Art of Doing Nothing (AODN) is more than telling your puppy to lie down; they need to understand that there are times when you want them to switch off and just chill out.

The AODN can happen anywhere at home. As they get older, you will start to introduce a dog bed and—depending on the kind of person you are—the sofa. (People ask me all the time if puppies should be allowed on the sofa or the bed, and the short answer is: it's up to you! There's a whole FAQ section at the back of the book that touches on this and other commonly asked questions.) Wherever it is that your dog chills out, this is where they need to understand the Art of Doing Nothing.

And it's not just for at home. The AODN is a useful skill to have wherever you are with your puppy. For example, you might take your puppy for a walk with a friend and decide to stop by the local pub for lunch on the way home. Being able to reliably know that you can enjoy your lunch without your puppy running around in circles and causing havoc is a beautiful thing, people. Teaching your dog this is basic good manners for them and for all the people you encounter on your daily travels—be it in a pub, on a train station platform, or a doctor's office waiting room—wherever other people are just getting on with their business and don't want to be terrorized by a crazy puppy!

Like the Art of Attention, the Art of Doing Nothing isn't a command you can train your dog to perform; it's a life skill for your puppy, and a concept you can keep in mind as we go through this training section. Got all of that? Awesome! Let's go.

Rewards

With most of my methods, you'll learn to use rewards to build motivation. Most often, this is going to be food from their daily allowance, but if you are worried about making that last, you don't want to have the treat pouch on you for some reason, or you just don't have access to decent treats, there are other ways to reward and motivate your puppy. Toys and puzzles can be equally pleasing to your puppy, so there's never any excuse for not rewarding the right behavior, guys!

If they get it wrong, be patient and understand that it's your job to teach them. They don't know sh*t about this human world! Remember, this is a blank canvas, and you are painting your masterpiece!

> **TIP:** *Use empty coffeepots or jam jars (or whatever the frik you like) to keep their food in different rooms around the house. This way, you're never going to run out of rewards! Just make sure you count it as part of their daily allowance.*

The Name Game

You will already have been saying your puppy's name to them a fair bit at this stage—I hope you have, anyway! So this shouldn't be a big thing, but let's just stop and think about what it actually means to them when we say it.

Your puppy doesn't think, "Oh, great, my name is Leo; I'm really pleased they called me Leo. That's my favorite name." And when he meets other dogs in the park, he doesn't go up to them and extend a paw and say, "Hi, mate, I'm Leo. How you doing?"

To your puppy, their name is a sound that usually tells them you need their attention, and that comes with a reward—at this stage. It's also a sound they will hear over and over for the rest of their lives. And like any of us hearing something over and over, puppies can become kind of desensitized to their name and lose the joy of hearing it. Worse, if their name is something they only hear in association with trouble, they'll start to fear and actively avoid the sound of it. This will make recall training very, very difficult.

When this happens, you begin to find that dogs stop paying attention to you when you say their name. And if you've got a dog who isn't interested when you say their name, you've got some serious training trouble on your hands, my friends. So my message here is to keep a positive tone in your voice when you say their name. Keep it light and fun. In a moment, we're going to look at other ways you can get, keep, and reward their attention (Just Say Yes), but for now your job is simply to keep that name giving them happy thoughts and feelings when you say it. And if you're not sure they've got it yet, go back over the technique we learned in chapter 4: Name. Reward. Name. Reward. Name. Reward, etc. Repeat until it sticks.

With a second dog in the house, it's important you use their individual names so they know you're talking to them. But once you've gotten their attention, you don't need to say their name repeatedly. It becomes a nag—and no one likes a nagging Nelly!

On your markers | Marker training and why it matters

Markers explained simply:

YES—Come to me to get your reward

GOOD—Continue doing what you're doing, I will come
to you to give you your reward

BREAK—Exercise is over—free dog

I use markers to train all my dogs, puppies, and adults alike. Never heard of marker training? Maybe you've heard of clickers? Some people like to use clickers, which are also markers, but I prefer to use spoken words. That way, I never find myself out without the clicker, plus I think it reinforces the bond between the dog and me. They respond to a voice more than a click. Anyway, the point is, I'm a big proponent of marker training, and the reason for this is simple: the difference between marker-trained dogs and non-marker-trained dogs is like night and day. A marker-trained dog understands at all times what is being asked of them. They do the right thing, you feel happy, they feel happy, and everyone's a winner.

So now I've sold it to you, you're probably thinking, "OK, what is marker training then?" Don't worry, you will not be drawing on your puppy with a Sharpie!

Markers are simply keywords that let your dog know they've done something good (like SIT) or they're currently doing something good (for example, DOWN), and they're going to get a reward. Markers help your dog understand what's expected of them. They give your dog clarity. You will be saying a marker word after every command you give your dog to reinforce its meaning. There are three markers listed below.

YES

YES is basically about rewarding your dog for doing the right thing.

Getting and maintaining their attention before you give them their favorite toy or food—anything they like—will ensure that you become the center of their universe. But puppies are busy little bees and easily distracted, so you need to learn and practice the art of getting and keeping their attention, guys. Practice this exercise until you can reliably say your puppy knows that looking at you is what needs to happen before any reward comes their way.

NOTE: YES is not a command or a request for them to do something; it's a confirmation that they have done what you wanted them to do, such as SIT or DOWN. I'm using SIT in this scenario because you have already taught your puppy to sit.

Introducing the YES marker:
- Get your dog's favorite food in your fingers.
- Tell your dog to SIT—wait for them to sit.
- Wait for them to look at you (direct eye contact required).
- Step back and say YES as you give your dog a treat to reward them.

Now that you've started introducing YES to your puppy's vocabulary, there are two other important marker words: GOOD and BREAK.

GOOD

This is what's called a duration marker. This means the dog is doing what you have asked them to do and you want them to continue doing it. Unlike YES, where your puppy comes to you for their reward and the behavior is over, with GOOD, you take the reward to them to encourage them to continue the good behavior, i.e., a duration sit.

BREAK

This is a signal that the exercise is over. Saying BREAK to your dog means they are free to go and do what they like for a bit.

To help you understand how marker words are used, here's a scenario where all three of them come into play:

1. Ask your puppy to SIT. Say GOOD (because you want the sit to continue) and take your dog a reward when their butt hits the floor. Sometimes you may have to repeat the command SIT to maintain the sit position (more on SIT on page 58).
2. When your puppy makes direct eye contact, say YES and step back, which will bring your pup out of the SIT as they come to you to get the reward. If you want to keep them in a SIT, say SIT, give them a treat, and then add GOOD (because you want them to continue sitting).

3. When you feel like your puppy has held the SIT long enough, say YES, step back, and reward the dog. If you want to let them know the exercise is over, say BREAK and throw a treat for them to go and find.

A simple way to remember your markers:
- YES: they come to you
- GOOD: you go to them
- BREAK: is a free dog

MARK AND REWARD a quick recap

Going forward, you're going to hear me telling you to mark and reward a lot. When your pup has done something you like, you need to mark it. Which marker word you use will depend on how you want them to behave. YES, come to you for a reward; GOOD, stay there while you go to them for a reward; BREAK, take a break and do their own thing for a bit.

Remember: always mark and reward a behavior you like!

Basic training (Sit, Down, Come, Heel, Leave It)

You need to know some basic commands so you can manage life safely and happily with both your puppy and the adult dog they will become. I will talk you through these one by one in a second, but I just want to flag that there is no linear approach here—you can practice any of these commands during any training session. They are all important, so be sure you mix them up and practice them equally during your puppy's daily routine.

Tone of voice

Your tone of voice is really important when it comes to training your puppy. Dogs tend to respond best to strong, single-syllable commands (that's why we say SIT to them, not "please be seated"). When your puppy has done something you've asked them to, you want to relay this in your tone of voice. This is when you can be high-pitched and happy in your tone.

However, when your puppy is unsure, or if you are communicating that you would like them to do something, try to deliver your words in a tone that leaves no room for doubt. I'm not saying you need to shout at them, but remember that dogs communicate in barks. I'm not asking you to bark—but again, remember that barks come in short, single-syllable bursts. Use a firm, short manner that lets them know what's being expected of them and you can get to the happy bit much quicker.

Body language

How you move and how your body occupies the space you and your dog share plays a massive part in how your puppy responds to you. On a simplistic level, asking your puppy to lie down but pointing up to the sky will send a confusing message to them. So try to always think about the signals you use when communicating with them. But more than this, body language is about your physical presence and what it represents to your pup. If you want your puppy to drop something or stop doing something, standing behind them, talking on the phone while you are waving at them, or generally making your presence smaller to them will probably not get your message across. Standing in front of them, firm and confident, so that they can see that you mean what you are saying lets them know this is a nonnegotiable request.

For example, if your puppy jumps up at you, you might instinctively move backward to get out of their way. This will get you out of their space for a few seconds, but it will never stop the jumping—you are simply making yourself a moving (and even more fun!) target for your puppy. Whereas, if you move forward and actually step into their space, you'll find that they stop jumping up at you. You have taken ownership of the space as opposed to giving it up by moving backward. Guys, let me be clear: heavy-handedness and physical aggression toward a puppy is NEVER OK. But you can use your body language to assert yourself and communicate with your puppy when you want them to do something.

SIT

This is probably the most basic command you will teach your pup, but it's also one of the most useful, and all dogs should know it.

You need SIT because you want to be able to keep your puppy in one place at times, perhaps because you want them to calm down before they do something else, or because you need to know they're in a safe place for a minute while you answer the door or whatever it is. SIT means they sit and should stay sitting until released or given further instructions. The stay is implied. I never use the word *stay*; it's unnecessary in dog training. "Sit" means sit, and "Down" means down. Let's not overcomplicate things by adding "Stay!"

Teaching SIT

With a treat in your fingers, hold it to your puppy's nose and slowly raise it above their head. As their head goes up, their butt should go down. Once this happens, wait for them to look at you, *mark and reward* with YES, step back, and give the dog a reward.

Notice how we have added the marker word YES to the command SIT. This lets your puppy know that they have done the right thing and can now have a reward. Once your dog is fluent in the SIT action, you can add in the duration marker GOOD (where they continue to hold the SIT until you come to them with the reward) to build the duration of the SIT. Sometimes you might want your puppy to remain in the SIT while you go to answer the door or pop out of sight for a moment for whatever reason. You can practice putting some distance between you and your puppy while they are doing SIT by trying this:

- Ask your puppy to SIT, take a step back, say GOOD, and give them a reward.

- Repeat this, but next time, take two steps back before you say GOOD.
- Next time, take three steps before you say GOOD, and so on.

When you have enough distance, wait for your puppy to look at you, say YES, and they will come running to you for the reward.

To put it simply: SIT   YES   REWARD

For a next-level exercise, introduce the other markers and rewards to your SIT practice: SIT—GOOD—BREAK.

DOWN

DOWN is one of the most important commands you will teach your puppy. Just as SIT means SIT until further notice, DOWN also means DOWN until you're released or given further instructions. DOWN is especially useful because if your pup knows DOWN means DOWN anywhere, you can use this to help them relax and understand what is happening in new environments, i.e., in the pub, in restaurants, at friends' houses, or outside a shop. It helps you and your puppy chill out in so many situations.

With your treat in your fingers, hold it to your puppy's nose and slowly lower the treat toward the floor. You may need to move the treat along the floor toward you, to encourage their butt to touch the floor. The moment their butt goes down and you are sure all four legs are down, say YES, step back, and reward your dog. Repeat.

Notice again how you have acknowledged their correct action with the marker word YES and rewarded them for doing the right thing. DOWN can be a tricky behavior to teach, guys. Make sure your dog is on a leash while you are teaching them. You can also apply very gentle pressure to their back and gentle leash guidance in a downward motion (and I really do mean gentle pressure—too much pressure, and your puppy will freak out and resist).

> **TIP:** *Remember your markers, guys! If you want to build the duration of DOWN (i.e., keep them there for longer) and/or build in some distance (i.e., walk into another room or to the door), use your GOOD marker word. When you feel they have been in DOWN for long enough, say YES, and they will come to you for their reward.*

To put it simply: DOWN   YES   REWARD

For a next-level exercise, introduce the other markers and rewards to your DOWN practice:

DOWN   GOOD   BREAK

COME (aka recall)

You have already been practicing this command without knowing it! The YES marker and your puppy's name suggest to your pup that they should come to you for a reward. So you have done some of the work already. COME is essential if you hope one day to have your puppy off the leash, running around in the woods or on the beach.

The trick with COME is to avoid setting yourself up to fail by trying to teach your dog in a situation when they can physically ignore you. Teach them this word when they are on a leash so that if they ignore you because they're distracted, you can gently pull the dog toward you to show them you want them to COME. This way, there are no negotiations.

To practice COME, simply call your dog's name and say COME; as soon as the dog starts to come toward you, mark it with YES and reward.

To put it simply: NAME. COME YES REWARD

KEY POINT: One of the most irresponsible things a dog owner can do is let their puppy off the leash with no recall; it puts your dog and others at risk every time you unclip that leash.

Leash walking

Being able to go for an enjoyable walk with your dog doesn't happen by magic—leash walking requires practice to make perfect. Many reactivity-based issues come about simply because your puppy has not learned how to behave on the leash when outside of your home. Proper leash walking teaches your puppy to be calm and to follow you (which will help with recall), and when done properly, it's a great bonding experience.

Reactivity in a dog is a catchall term for when they react to certain simulations or stimuli. It's not about aggression, although it can show up as this in some dogs if not handled correctly. Reactivity can look like barking, lunging, crouching down in a stalkerish kind of a position, whining, chewing—it can be anything that seems out of the ordinary. Your dog can be reactive to humans or other animals, or it can be reactive to certain environments or sounds—it all depends on the dog and their genetics, socialization experiences, and pretty much everything else.

As I've already said, with a puppy you have a blank canvas on which to paint your masterpiece. My training methods with puppies are all about preventing reactivity and avoiding those difficult behaviors before they set in. Why? Because as I'm writing this, Leo (the massive Rottweiler who you see on the cover of this book) is chilling out at my feet, just doing his own thing while I work, not bothering me or feeling stressed about anything. He's happy in his own skin and feels safe and secure. This hasn't happened by magic; it's because we have done everything that I am teaching you in this book. So keep reading!

Now, with teaching a puppy leash walking, I don't believe in being overly strict. I'm not looking for that militant-looking walk with the dog walking perfectly by my side, staring up at my face the whole time. The main focus at this stage should be on allowing the pup to explore and take in the world, to build their knowledge and confidence. So my only real requirement with puppy leash walking is for them not to pull.

When they get to the adolescent mark at around six months, you can start adding in a lot more structure, like having your puppy walk by your side at HEEL for ten minutes or so before allowing the dog time to sniff and explore as a reward—we'll come to the HEEL command and adding structure later on in Adolescence on page 102.)

So, guys, here's the thing—the easiest way to stop your dog from pulling as you walk is to not reinforce pulling. By this I mean if you continue to move forward (walk) while they're putting tension on the leash (pulling), your puppy will quickly learn that pulling creates a forward motion—and you are basically reinforcing pulling. So stop leash pulling with a puppy.

I want you to follow this simple rule: you stop when there is tension on the leash.

When you feel your puppy's leash go slack, you mark and reward with YES and lure them to your left side with a treat and then continue to move forward. (This is known as free shaping. We're teaching them to heel before we even say the word to them.) Repeat this as much as necessary, even if you are in a rush or feel like an idiot standing in the road or stopping every two steps. Stop caring about everyone else's thoughts and focus on what your puppy needs to learn. The only reason this method doesn't work is that people are not patient enough to stop every time until their puppy learns not to pull. But remember, what might take you an hour today will take you 50 minutes tomorrow, then 45, and so forth until it becomes second nature to your puppy.

A few more leash walking tips:

- For the best results, practice leash walking inside the house at first, ideally in a non-distracting environment like a hallway (not a room full of food or children).
- Try to ensure your puppy is calm when they see the leash (no jumping around or getting excited—that goes for you and the dog).
- Work on your puppy's understanding of thresholds before leaving the house.
- If you have a very energetic dog, a quick play session with a ball or flirt pole before the walk will get out some of their pent-up energy and make for an easier walk.
- Once your puppy has their vaccinations and you start going out with them, master walking up and down your street before taking them to a completely new and distracting environment (like a dog park).

LEAVE IT

Again, LEAVE IT is one of the most important things to teach your puppy; this can be the difference between life and death. The average home is full of small items just waiting for a puppy to chew and choke on. Phone chargers, hairbrushes, shoes . . . you get the idea. And when you begin to get out and about, the potential for disaster only increases. Imagine being with your puppy and he picks up a cooked chicken bone but doesn't understand what LEAVE IT means. Things could very quickly go south for your pup. Every single dog on the planet must understand what LEAVE IT means; there are no exceptions.

To teach LEAVE IT, I like to use things the dog can't have, like a kid's toy. Soft toys like small teddy bears are great because they also look like small animals, making them doubly desirable to your curious puppy. Begin with your puppy on the leash and let them know you've got the toy, then throw it a short distance, somewhere they can still see it. They will instantly try to run over to investigate the flying teddy. Use your leash to gently hold your puppy back and say the words LEAVE IT as you prevent them from getting to the toy. As soon as you feel the leash relax—meaning they have stopped trying to reach the toy—use the marker YES to let them know they have done the right thing, and they can come to you for a reward.

Rinse and repeat with many different items in different areas of the home, and for best results, practice this at random times so that your dog understands this command applies in all situations.

Thresholds

Thresholds are doors, gates, car trunks, crates, driveways, and any exit or entry your dog will pass through in its lifetime. It is extremely important, and for me as a trainer nonnegotiable, that you teach dogs how to respect thresholds. The rule here is plain and simple: an open door does NOT mean your puppy can automatically run through it. Thresholds are quite a complex concept for your puppy to grasp. We live in homes with rooms that have doorways and entrances where, most of the time, you don't need to prevent them from moving freely through them (unless you especially want to). But front doors, back gates, crates, car doors/trunks, and any new environments that can pose a potential danger—or cause chaos on the other side—are a must-train. If you live near a road, failure to establish a clear understanding of thresholds could result in injury or even death of your beloved new puppy.

Teaching thresholds

Make sure your puppy is on their long training leash so that if they somehow make it past you, you can be sure they are safe.

Stand between your puppy and the threshold you are working on (a back door onto a garden is ideal for this initial training as you don't risk your puppy being distracted or tempted by traffic or passersby). Slowly open the door and then, if your pup goes to move forward, close the door.

Repeat this. Your aim is to have your puppy remain in their position while you open the door.

Wait for their eye contact (art of attention), and then, if it is safe and you are ready, walk through the threshold while giving further instructions (saying "Let's go" or something similar to allow a slow release).

> **TIP:** *There are plenty of times when an open door won't mean walkies are imminent. Maybe you are picking up a parcel that's been left on the front step or you've opened the car trunk to put something in but don't want them to jump out and run off into the distance. Practice opening doors at random times without actually letting your dog pass through the threshold.*

Grooming

Grooming is an essential part of training your puppy, and there are no exceptions. This is not about putting their hair in a bow or giving them fluffy ankles; it's about giving your puppy the basic care and maintenance they need. It's also about helping them learn to be comfortable with being handled.

Dogs come in all shapes and sizes, so your puppy's breed will play a big part in their grooming requirements. A Border terrier with a thick, wiry coat and oily follicles that can become blocked and irritated will need to be hand-stripped. This is where the groomer removes the dead hairs from their coat by hand instead of clippers. However, a breed with a shorter, smoother coat, like a Staffordshire bull terrier, will be fine with just a quick brush when it comes to coat maintenance.

Grooming is a real craft, and a decent dog groomer can make life a lot easier for you, especially with a dog whose coat needs a lot of maintenance. I recommend you find yourself a good groomer as soon as you get your puppy (they can start being groomed as soon as they've had their second round of vaccinations, around ten to twelve weeks). Don't forget to build those costs into the picture when you are weighing up the affordability of a dog, folks. This is an essential service, so you can't skimp on it. The good news is it can save you money on vets' fees in the long run, because a good groomer (along with a healthy balanced diet) will help prevent many of the problems associated with skin and coat maintenance. So it balances out.

Of course, successful grooming is a two-way street. A good groomer is worth their weight in gold, but it will always help them do their job better if you can raise a desensitized puppy, by which I mean one that is completely chilled out about being handled. So, before your puppy goes to the groomer, they should ideally be happy to be handled all over, have their paws and tails held, their coats brushed, and used to having human hands in areas such as their mouth and ears.

It's easy to introduce basic grooming to your pup from the get-go, and you should aim to set aside time for mini-grooming sessions, where you practice stroking, touching, holding, and brushing your puppy. If they've got floppy ears, you can gently lift them, as well as lifting their top lip to get them used to the idea that, sometimes, you want to look at their teeth. Do all of this in very short sessions with lots and lots of rewards and praise—again, this is always made easier if you are hand-feeding your dog. But not to worry if you aren't hand-feeding; high-quality training treats will help do the job!

Grooming is also a great opportunity to check for any abnormal lumps and bumps, which if found you should let your vet know about immediately. Your vet will also appreciate your efforts with grooming—a dog who is not accustomed to being handled can find visits to the vet extremely stressful and traumatic.

What about washing?

It's easy to assume that dirty dogs need to be washed and bathed, but washing their coats with products can be detrimental to your puppy's coat and can actually mean you have to wash them more frequently. Dogs have natural oils in their coats that help keep them clean; too much bathing strips the oils, leaving the hair more susceptible to damage, and making them look lackluster. It's a vicious cycle. Dogs just don't need shampoo, guys!

A decent, balanced diet will ensure your puppy's coat looks great. If they get covered in mud, and you really need to clean them up, a simple wash with lukewarm water and a good brush is all they need.

Claws: to trim or not?

As with their coats, puppies' claws are pretty self-regulating, and for most of them, daily exposure to pavements, patios, and other hard surfaces is enough to keep them in check (my Rottweiler, Daisy, was a senior before we ever had to trim her claws). However, sometimes their claws can get a bit long and make life difficult for you when handling them as they can scratch.

Long, uncomfortable claws can also affect their foot placement and the way they walk, and occasionally a dew claw (the big toe/thumb claw located farther up the limb) can be loosely attached, so it's always worth keeping an eye on your puppy's claws and dealing with any problems swiftly. You can buy claw trimmers for dogs, but I recommend you let your groomer do this if needed. A wrong clip can lead to bleeding and a traumatic experience for your pup. This is a job that is better left to the experts, especially when puppies are young and wriggly!

CHAPTER 6

Putting Your Training into the Real World

By the time your puppy is 12 weeks old, they should have had their second round of vaccinations—this means it's safe for them to get out and about in the real world, and your adventures together can really begin! The first and most important thing you need to do at this stage is to keep your expectations low. Remember, you can't expect perfect puppy obedience straight off the bat here. For now, I want you to focus on making all of these first experiences feel positive and motivating for your pup.

First walk

Your puppy's first walks out in the world will be a sensory overload. All the new sights, sounds, smells, and sensations are likely overwhelming, so take it slow! You will already have been practicing leash walking in the house, and your puppy should be accustomed to the leash being on. An ideal first walk would be to simply continue the leash walking you've already been doing by walking up and down your road or around the grounds of your apartment.

If your pup stops, let them stop. If your pup wants to sniff, let them sniff. If you feel like your pup is scared or panicking (they might be shaking or physically cowering or whimpering), try to let them go through the motions and find their confidence. Please, do not mollycoddle your puppy! Don't talk in a baby voice to them, stroke them, or pick them up if and when they look scared. Instead, simply take a deep breath, shorten the leash, wait for your puppy to check in with you (eye contact), and then carry on with your walk. Your puppy has learned to stay calm through moments of fear, and the art of attention has let them know you have their back.

Mark and reward: During your first few walks in the world with your puppy, make sure you mark and reward any good behaviors you ask for, or that your puppy presents to you voluntarily, especially the art of attention. If they are regularly checking in and making eye contact with you, reward that with a YES or a GOOD and a treat to let them know you like this behavior.

Poo bags: Don't forget your poo bags, people, and always clean up after your dog. When your puppy goes to the toilet when you are on a walk, always mark and reward them. This way, they learn that good things happen when they do their business while they are out and about, and you have less poo to deal with in your back garden.

New places

As your puppy becomes more confident outside, you can start taking them to new places. Because owning a dog isn't always about going on long walks at the beach or in the countryside; you might need to walk your dog with you alongside the stroller on the school run or take them in the car when you pop over to the supermarket. Many tradespeople take their dogs to work, so their puppies need to get used to being in the van. If you care for an elderly relative, your puppy needs to know their house. I've put together a checklist of new and familiar places to expose your puppy to.

Practice, practice, practice!

As with their first walks, you mustn't expect miracles when you put your puppy in these new places for the first time. With puppies, it's all about patience and repetition. Take the time to practice all the things you have been working on indoors at these new places so that your puppy doesn't only associate them with being at home. SIT, DOWN, LEAVE IT, and COME can all be worked on at the park or waiting at the school gate or wherever you are. Keep the marker words and rewards coming and watch as your puppy's confidence grows and grows.

Short and sweet

Please remember that your puppy is still a baby at this stage. You wouldn't expect a baby to go on long walks as soon as they take their first steps! In the same way, you can't expect your puppy to keep going for hours all day with you just because they've now had all their vaccinations. So as with your indoor training sessions, keep your new adventures in the real world short and sweet for now, and always build in plenty of time for your puppy to rest. As with humans, rest is crucial for their growth, and it's when they download all that new information they're taking in all the time. Remember, you've got a whole lifetime with this animal by your side; there is plenty of time!

Other dogs

As you begin to get out and about with your puppy, there is one thing you are definitely going to come across that they are going to be extremely interested in (or extremely scared of), and that is other dogs. Once you become a dog owner, you notice that dogs are EVERYWHERE. And if you are at the park or in an area where people walk their dogs a lot, you will encounter many adult dogs who are not on leashes. For many puppies, the sight of an adult dog bounding over to them at high speed can be terrifying and lead to long-term fear of other dogs. As your puppy's only source of protection and confidence, you need to prevent this from happening.

Have their back

I hear it over and over, "It's OK, they're friendly!" People let their off-leash dog come running over to yours, and it starts sniffing around or humping your dog and jumping all over them. When people shout this to me as their dog invades my dog's space, I always know that what they are really saying is that they can't control their dog. Someone shouting "It's OK, they're friendly!" from across the park is shouting this because their dog has no recall—their dog is basically not trained, and their dog's face up your puppy's butt is risky business.

As soon as you see an adult dog bounding over to your puppy, I want you to put your puppy behind you and form a protective shield between your puppy and the other dog. A stern stamp of the foot and (if you're like me) a firm "F*ck off" should deter the off-leash dog. But if it isn't enough to shoo the other dog away, you have to be prepared to grab and push them away. Your new puppy is forming trust with you, and the quickest way to destroy that trust is for you to allow them to have a bad experience when you are meant to be looking out for them.

Mind your manners

Ideally, other dog owners should ask if it is OK for their dog to come and say hello to your puppy. If someone has been well-mannered enough to ask this, and providing their dog seems to be calm and under control—and if it's something you actually want to happen—then by all means allow them to come and say hello.

Use the three-second rule

I always like to keep to the three-second rule while out with a young puppy. It massively reduces the risk of them having a bad experience.

Here's an example: the owner of an off-leash dog has asked if their dog can come over and say hello to your puppy. You have agreed, but it's the first time your puppy has met such a big dog and you're not sure what will happen. They start sniffing each other. Count in your head for three seconds: 1, 2, 3. Call your puppy back to you and use your leash as a lure if they don't come back at first. Mark and reward them for returning to you, even while a new dog distracted them. If they seemed to like the other dog, there is nothing to stop you from reintroducing them in a few minutes.

Keeping it short and sweet with the three-second rule ensures that none of the dogs become overstimulated, and you don't end up with two wildly hyper dogs bowling over each other. It also teaches your young puppy the importance of impulse control and the need to respond to you (the art of attention, guys!) even when distracted by a big, exciting new friend. And it ensures that you remain your puppy's favorite thing. Other dogs can very quickly become more fun than you, and if this notion builds and builds over time, you can end up with a dog who is always more interested in other dogs than you. Remember, your focus between now and adolescence (roughly six months of age) should be on having fun with your dog as you work through the socialization checklist.

A word about fear imprints

Before we jump into socialization, I just want to tell you about fear imprint periods. Never heard of a puppy fear imprint period? It is really important that you know about these! A fear imprint period is something that happens to a puppy, usually between eight to eleven weeks old, and just around the time you are bringing them home. It can happen twice in some dogs— usually, the second time comes around six months. During these imprint periods, your dog can become spooked by the strangest things. My Rottweiler, Daisy, got really freaked out by statues and overflowing garbage cans, while a Patterdale terrier I know was terrified of gates. They can become irrationally scared of all sorts of stuff, but the important thing to remember is that the thing that is freaking them out isn't the issue. What matters is your response to it.

We can screw dogs up in these important periods of their lives by making a big deal of whatever it is they are scared of, avoiding certain situations, or mollycoddling the dog and pulling them close when they get scared. Your efforts to reassure a dog who is scared of a kid's bike by pulling them back and telling them it's OK might make sense to you, but to the dog it only amplifies their sense of caution and fear. They learn to be afraid of the bike and continue to bark and growl at every kid on a bike they see, forevermore. Not ideal.

Remember: I would be out of a job if telling a dog "It's OK" was enough. You wouldn't need a dog trainer.

In these moments, we need to laugh off the fear, play it down, and give them the confidence they need. When I realized that Daisy was scared of a massive statue of a doughnut at my local sea life center, I walked confidently with her back and forth in front of it, ignoring her whimpers until eventually she got the idea that this giant piece of confectionery wasn't going to kill her. She went on to become one of the most confident dogs I've ever known.

GOLDEN RULE: If your puppy is acting scared of something, do not try to "comfort" them in the way you might a human being. Instead, lead by example and show them they have nothing to fear. Slow down and take deep breaths. It's a phase—don't overthink it.

Socialization—what is it?

Socialization is about teaching your dog how to be comfortable and content in the real world, be it around humans, other dogs, noises, smells, or any other distractions they may encounter. Proper socialization is incredibly important, as a dog who doesn't feel confident and relaxed around new people and experiences can become fearful and reactive, and this leads to all sorts of problems that you really don't need in your life.

So, as far as I'm concerned, all dogs must be properly and

thoroughly socialized; there are no exceptions. A lot of people think socializing a puppy means they just need to take their dog out a lot and let it meet loads of people and other dogs, and that will be fine. But contrary to this belief, letting your puppy meet everything and everyone it comes across is not what socialization is about. Socialization is something that needs to be approached seriously as a key part of your puppy's training schedule. For that reason, I like to break it down into three key areas that can easily be worked through. These are: environmental, animal, and human. Let's have a closer look.

Environmental socialization

Environmental doesn't only mean taking your pup out to plenty of different places and spaces—although this is massively important. It's also about letting them experience different kinds of weather, temperatures, and terrains—so, yes, that means you've got to get your gear on and get outside even when it's pouring!

One of the big mistakes I regularly see people make with their dogs is to only take them to the same place every day. How boring is that! It is not only unfulfilling for you and the dog, but it is also not helping your dog learn how to be cool in new situations. Sure, you might think you've got a dog who is well-behaved in the field you take them to every day. But if that field of grass is the only place they ever go to outside of their home, your dog is going to totally lose their sh*t if you take them to a new park or field one day. They will be so absorbed in the new experience that they will struggle to pay attention to you (remember the Art of Attention?). And that, my friends, is when things start to go wrong.

Proper environmental exposure is about taking your dog to many different places and letting them see, feel, and experience as many different sights, sounds, and smells as possible. It's about getting out in the rain, snow, wind, and sunshine, walking through muddy fields and busy town centers, along open beaches, and through thick, dense woods. It's also about pubs, shops, buses, and just about anywhere else you can think of that you'll be taking your puppy, no matter how frequently or infrequently.

We've all seen, and probably laughed at, dogs who are afraid to walk through puddles and across certain surfaces, or dogs who are terrified of loud bangs or heavy traffic. Whatever it is they're scared of, it's because they were never exposed to these things (socialized) at a young age. You are building their confidence and character by taking your dog to all these new places and allowing them to take in the world through their nose at their own pace. And remember, socialization is something you can do at the same time as all the obedience training that you learned in chapter 5. The more you can practice your SIT, DOWN, COME, and LEAVE IT commands in new and different places, the more able to function in any situation your dog will be.

Take a look at the checklist on page 87 and simply work your way through it by taking your puppy for walks to all of the places mentioned.

Tip: If your pup gets nervous in a new place, don't panic. Don't mollycoddle them and for f*ck's sake don't tell them "It's

OK" like they understand what that means! In the nicest sense, in this situation, I really just want you to shut the f*ck up! When your puppy freaks out, people tend to try to humanize them and reassure them, but this only worsens things. You need to stop for a second, shorten your puppy's leash, take a deep breath, wait for the dog to stop panicking, and then move on. This way, the fear doesn't win and your puppy's ability to handle strange and stressful situations grows.

City dogs and country dogs—a few things to consider

Your puppy's breed and characteristics often stem from the environment they were originally bred to work and thrive in. Terriers and collies are dogs who worked the land, Labradors were bred for assistance, and lapdogs for looking nice on someone's lap. If you live in a busy city and find yourself in possession of a big St. Bernard—a dog originally bred for Alpine rescues—it's a good idea to make sure they are given at least some opportunities to fulfill their breed's instincts and experience the environments they are designed to thrive in. With a St. Bernard, you might make hilly walks a priority, and with a terrier, let them access some outdoor terrain where they can really put their speed and determination to good use. Equally, a small dog with little legs and a lack of stamina, like a miniature dachshund or a Chihuahua, is not going to love long muddy walks in the country, so walks along nice even pavements where they can get into their stride are going to be more enjoyable for them.

Wherever you live, if you have a city dog, it is important you teach them how to behave in rural settings, and if you live in the country, make sure your dog experiences urban settings occasionally. Even if these are not regular situations for them, it all gets them more prepared for certain situations.

Animal socialization

You might automatically assume this means getting your puppy used to other dogs, which is a large part of it, but it's more about helping your dog know how to behave in the presence of other animals, including dogs. There are a lot of animals about! Especially if you live somewhere rural where animals like horses, cows, and sheep are a regular part of daily life. But even in the most urban setting, there are a surprising number of animals in our everyday lives, from other domestic pets like cats and hamsters, to the birds we see in the park, as well as the foxes who come into our gardens at night. So it's not enough to just take your dog to the park and let them play with every dog they come across, thinking that you are somehow socializing them.

In fact, allowing your puppy to go up to every dog you meet and play with every dog whose path you cross is the opposite of what we want to achieve here. Letting them be "free range" might sound cool, but that is actually how many reactivity issues are formed. Your puppy might be the most placid dog on the planet, but if they come across a dog who is unpleasant to them, or they have a bad experience with another dog in the park, that will stay with them for good. You are not protecting your puppy if you expose them to these dangers. What I want you to achieve isn't some kind of social-butterfly puppy, but instead a socially ignorant pup. Yes, folks, I want your puppy to be able to happily ignore other dogs and animals, not leap around all over them.

Why do I say this? Well, think about why you got this puppy in the first place. Was it so you could have a companion or so you could watch them tear all over the park with someone else's dog? Remember, it's man's best friend, not everyone else's dog's best friend. You get a dog for you and your family. If you let your dog expect to be able to play with every other dog you meet, you're not going to be spending that much time with them when you're out and about, and their sense of loyalty to you will become diluted.

Through establishing social ignorance, other dogs become less interesting to your puppy. Your pup becomes calm in the presence of other dogs. Social ignorance also applies to other animals you might encounter, like horses and sheep. Once you feel that your pup is suitably ignorant (I know, it sounds weird!), you can start introducing them to the dogs and other animals YOU want them to meet.

Danger: "It's OK, they're friendly!"

If a dog comes tearing across the field with its owner screaming, "It's OK, they're friendly!," from half a mile away, be very cautious. They are saying this because they know their COME command isn't going to work. If that's not in place, how do you know what will happen when your puppy meets their out-of-control dog? Steer clear of dogs and owners who can't deliver on the basic commands. The dogs you should be looking to introduce your dog to should be those owned by family and friends, the dogs you will be spending time with in the future.

Establishing social ignorance in your puppy

Keep your dog's social circle small. Allow them to play with and meet the dogs in your own social circle, who you know you will be spending time with over the years. If you don't have a lot of dogs in your circle of family and friends, joining a training club that offers controlled socializing is a great way to get your puppy used to other dogs.

- Follow the socialization checklist to ensure your pup has met and been exposed to all the other animals on the list.
- As with fear imprints, keep your puppy on the leash when they are meeting new animals and practice your Art of Attention skills, guys! When a new and interesting dog comes bounding up to your pup, I want you to break your pup's focus on the other dog. Bring out a favorite tug toy or practice any of your obedience commands (SIT, DOWN, etc.), and mark and reward to let your puppy know you are pleased with them for paying attention to you and not the other dog.
- You need to do this consistently whenever you encounter

a potentially distracting other dog. Eventually, your pup will learn that you are the best option every time there's a choice between you and another dog.

And remember: your puppy doesn't need dog "friends" to be happy. Dogs don't do friends, people! This is anthropomorphism! Your puppy only needs YOU.

Human socialization

This is not that different from animal socialization when it comes down to it. How do I mean? Human socialization for your dog is not just about letting everyone who wants to say hello to your cute puppy come and say hello. Why? Because a teenage girl rushing over and saying in a high-pitched voice, "OMG, I LOVE PUPPIES," and cuddling them is not really the kind of human you want to introduce your puppy to every five minutes. This kind of baby talk can either scare the sh*t out of your puppy and be a negative experience or create sheer over-arousal and an overexcitable pup who thinks it's OK to go la-la every time it meets a human being.

Remember: socialization is about quality over quantity. You want to work on teaching your puppy to ignore strange people (social ignorance, guys). If someone wants to say hello and you are happy for them to do so, make sure your puppy is in a SIT stay and is calm before letting the stranger say hello.

TIP: *Go through the checklist below and make sure you introduce your puppy calmly to the people on the list. Items of clothing like hoods, big bags, hats, and unusual hairstyles can all freak a puppy out, so it's important that you go out of your way to get them in front of people wearing these things and, as with other animals, demonstrate your own calm confidence to reassure your puppy about how to behave.*

Socialization checklist

Unfamiliar people

- [ ] wearing backpacks
- [ ] dancing
- [ ] running
- [ ] riding a bike
- [ ] different ethnicities
- [ ] men with beards
- [ ] men with deep voices
- [ ] tall people
- [ ] wearing hats
- [ ] wearing sunglasses
- [ ] toddlers
- [ ] infants
- [ ] teenagers
- [ ] elderly
- [ ] children playing
- [ ] clowns
- [ ] walking with canes or walkers

Meeting animals

- [ ] puppies
- [ ] old dogs
- [ ] male adult dogs
- [ ] female adult dogs
- [ ] different breeds
- [ ] different temperaments
- [ ] flat-faced dogs
- [ ] kittens
- [ ] cats
- [ ] horses
- [ ] pocket pets
- [ ] farm animals
- [ ] squirrels
- [ ] rabbits
- [ ] birds
- [ ] cows
- [ ] forest animals
- [ ] ducks

Sights and sounds

- [ ] sirens
- [ ] fireworks
- [ ] car horns
- [ ] motorbikes
- [ ] thunderstorms
- [ ] wheelchairs
- [ ] cars
- [ ] trucks
- [ ] doorbells
- [ ] skateboards
- [ ] airplanes
- [ ] vacuum cleaner
- [ ] hair dryer
- [ ] alarm
- [ ] washing machine
- [ ] crowds of people

Body handling

- [ ] checking the ears
- [ ] opening the eyelids
- [ ] handling and trimming nails
- [ ] grooming brush
- [ ] touching tail
- [ ] touching belly
- [ ] squeezing paws
- [ ] bending toward puppy
- [ ] grabbing the collar
- [ ] hugging your puppy
- [ ] holding/cradling in your arms

Places

- [ ] parks
- [ ] lakes
- [ ] forests
- [ ] bridges
- [ ] shopping areas
- [ ] boarding kennel
- [ ] day care
- [ ] pet shop
- [ ] vet
- [ ] groomer
- [ ] night-time
- [ ] dog-friendly
  - [ ] classes
  - [ ] events
  - [ ] restaurants

Objects and terrain

- [ ] pots and pans
- [ ] brooms
- [ ] umbrellas
- [ ] balloons
- [ ] bags blowing in the wind
- [ ] road signs
- [ ] garbage cans
- [ ] benches
- [ ] escalators
- [ ] elevators
- [ ] tile floors
- [ ] wood floors
- [ ] carpet
- [ ] stairs
- [ ] wet grass

CHAPTER 7

Common Mistakes and Practices

Now you're getting out and about with your puppy and feeling more confident about how to manage them, it's a good moment to stop and do a bit of troubleshooting. No one gets everything right all the time, guys, myself included! So let's look at some of the most common mistakes we all make when raising our puppies and see if we can work through some of them together. These are mistakes I've personally made or common problems my clients at Southend Dog Training come up against and regularly ask me about.

Taking your puppy to the same place

I can't believe how many people I see doing this: taking their puppy on the same walk, to the same place, at the same time every single day. What is that about?! Not only is it massively dull for your puppy, folks, but it can also cause reactivity. They learn to become comfortable in this one setting or routine, but as soon as you take them somewhere new, they revert to "factory settings" and struggle to pay attention to you because of the sensory overload of a new place. Mix up your walking routines with different places and ensure you are ticking off all the places on the environmental socialization checklist—and add a few more of your own if you can.

Letting everyone say hello to your puppy

You can miss the fact that your puppy is uncomfortable and/or overstimulated when someone else is making a fuss over them. Remember, it is all about quality over quantity when your pup meets someone new for the first time. Remember: "It's OK, they're friendly!" is an excuse that people who haven't trained their dogs use for their lack of control.

Stroking your puppy when it is doing something you don't like

This is probably one of the most common mistakes people make with puppies. To puppies, stroking is a reward. It's fuss and approval from you. So if your puppy jumps up and you stroke them, you're rewarding them. If they are reacting to another dog somehow and you stroke them because you think it will calm them down, you are effectively rewarding their unwanted behavior. So always take a few seconds before you stroke your puppy and ask yourself, What am I rewarding?

Telling your dog "It's OK" when they are worried

If telling your puppy "It's OK" worked every time they got worried about something, then you would not be reading this book, and we wouldn't need dog trainers. The fact is that dogs do not understand the nuances of the English language the way we do, folks. So when you say "It's OK" to your puppy who is cowering in fear at the giant poodle who's trying to hump them, you are basically talking nonsense to your dog and increasing their confusion and worry at the same time. If you think your puppy needs your protection or reassurance, show them with your body language (firm, confident pose) and by using words you know they understand. These should be your commands and your marker words. Everything else is irrelevant to them.

Good days and bad days

You're going to have both; that's a given. You are not building a robot dog, guys. You are working with a sophisticated animal with a brain who cannot always be predictable and will undoubtedly throw you curveballs. Chewed furniture, dog sh*t, whining . . . whatever it is, I know from experience that it can feel overwhelming sometimes, especially if you're already juggling a busy work and family life. I want you to remember that it's not about avoiding difficult situations, it's about how you handle them that will largely dictate how your dog—and your relationship with them—turns out. It's OK to have a bad day when your dog doesn't seem to be manageable and you wonder why the hell you got them in the first place. We've all been there.

When it happens, just stop for a second, ask yourself what went wrong that day and how you can learn from it . . . and move on. Concentrate on the good days; don't let the bad days overshadow all the good days.

Letting your puppy off the leash too soon

This is probably the most irresponsible thing any dog owner can do. Why? Because the reality is, if you let your puppy off the leash and it is not yet properly trained, you are putting your puppy's life and the lives of others—humans and dogs—at risk. A puppy on the road is a potential car crash situation, with far more risk to life than just the puppy's. You also set your dog up to fail when you let them off the leash too soon. If you let your puppy off and it ignores you, you are essentially giving them the green light to ignore you! Leashes are there to help us maintain control during the training stages; they are not optional.

Too much freedom before it is earned

What do I mean by too much freedom? Being left to their own devices too much, being ignored and under-managed. Puppies need guidance; I can't say that enough. Similarly to letting your puppy off the leash too soon, too much freedom too soon can be overwhelming for a young pup and lead to unwanted behaviors, such as stealing or destroying things. A puppy who feels lost will also follow you from room to room and have broken sleep, all behaviors that can manifest as separation anxiety and other anxious behaviors.

Having (too) high expectations

Although it's great to have high expectations for your puppy and how they will behave, it's also important to understand and accept that you will not have the perfect dog straight off the bat. Expecting your puppy to do a perfect HEEL on their first walk is a massively unreal expectation and only leaves everyone feeling disappointed, especially your puppy. Like all relationships, trust and understanding are built over time and with plenty of hard work. That's why it's important to do your training sessions and stick to your puppy's routine daily. It is in these moments that the foundation of your relationship is built.

Anthropomorphizing (treating your dog like a human)

Dogs are dogs, people! Assigning them human emotions and treating them like humans is deeply futile and incredibly detrimental to the dog. To be clear, I'm not saying dogs are "less than" humans; I'm saying they're not remotely human at all. Treating them like our children or our friends—I'm looking at you, the people who get them all dressed up, throw them birthday parties, and drive them around in their own cars—leaves them very confused! Remember: humans start wars, lie, cheat, and steal.

Why would you want to treat them like that? Dogs are pure, honest, and loyal to their core. What you see is absolutely what you get. Remember that before you start treating your puppy like a baby.

Separation anxiety: what is it and how to prevent it

Separation anxiety is a massive problem for a lot of people and their puppies, especially since the lockdowns of the coronavirus pandemic in 2020–2021. Thousands of people brought puppies into their lives while they were furloughed or working from home, only to find they had to leave them at home alone for hours on end once things got back to normal. Puppies don't understand the concept of jobs or popping out for a while, and they struggle to remember that even though you go away sometimes, you do come back. Separation anxiety can appear in many different ways. It can be more severe for some dogs than others, but either way, a pup experiencing this is a distressed animal who can whine, cry, defecate, destroy, and chew anything in its path when in the throes of an anxiety attack.

In theory, if you have followed everything in this book to the letter, you should find yourself with a puppy who is totally chill about being left on their own for periods of time. How come? Because you will have trained them to spend time in their crate, where they feel safe and secure. You will have taught them the Art of Doing Nothing—the idea that you expect and endorse them switching off occasionally means they can "engage" AODN when they find themselves home alone.

However, as I said, no one gets this sh*t perfect every time, not even me. So if you find your puppy is crying a lot when you go out, maybe they're having toilet accidents and chewing sh*t up, or worse, the neighbors are complaining about them barking while you're out, here are a couple of things you can do to halt this anxiety taking hold for the long term.

Revisit your crate training

If you are still carrying around any ideas about crates being "prisons" or somehow cruel for your dog, now is the time to lose those misconceptions once and for all. Dogs like to take shelter in nest-like environments—you see this behavior in street dogs in countries where dogs aren't so domesticated. Instead of shelters, we have crates in our homes, which can be a reassuring, safe space for your dog.

You will have been using a crate from day one of your training with me, but if for any reason it has slipped and you notice you're not using the crate as much as you were, double down on your crate training. Go back to page 38 and go over your puppy routine, making sure you always put your puppy in their crate after a good training session when they are tired.

TIP: *Do not just chuck your puppy in the crate every time you go out and expect them to be fine about that. All that is teaching them is that when you close the door on the crate, you p*ss off and don't come back for ages. It is really important that you put them in the crate at times when you are at home so that they understand it's just a safe place for them to chill out and doesn't mean instant abandonment.*

Consider how much you fuss over your puppy

If you are in a situation where your puppy gets stressed when you leave them, consider how much fuss you are making of them at home. (Remember, this is a measure for if and when your puppy has separation anxiety. I'm not saying everyone should automatically ration their affection, but if leaving them is becoming a problem, it could be that your puppy is overly dependent on being stroked and petted every time they are in your personal space.) It is perfectly OK to ignore your dog sometimes when they are around you and keep affection on your terms. Make a fuss about them as a reward for good behavior, not an automatic reflex because they're cute. This way, your puppy learns physical connection doesn't always happen every time you're next to them or nearby; they become more able to self-soothe.

Bring out the toys

Toys that are mentally enriching for your puppy, such as KONGs and LickiMats, can be a real help with separation anxiety. Giving them something to do while you are away that is engaging and distracting means their focus moves away from you (or the lack of you) and to the task at hand. Put some of your puppy's daily food allowance into a KONG, and suddenly your leaving becomes associated with food and dinnertime. A negative has become a positive!

Make sure they are exercised

There's no getting around the fact that a tired dog needs to rest, so if you can, try to schedule your departure for a time shortly after exercise or a training session. Put them in their crate, leave them with a KONG to work on, and suddenly being left becomes a pleasurable opportunity for them to rest and chill, not abandoning a dog bursting with surplus energy.

Remove your emotions

This is easier said than done; however, if you are panicking that your dog will get stressed because you are leaving, your dog will pick up on this, which will only contribute further to your dog's stress. Dogs are very black-and-white in the way they think. They don't realize you're stressing about leaving them, and they don't have the capacity for this kind of empathy. They just know that you left all stressed, which freaks them out more. So when you have to leave your dog, leave without emotion or hesitation and act as if nothing is happening.

With all of these measures in place, you should quite quickly see a reduction in any separation anxiety your puppy is experiencing. You might find over time that you can ease your foot off the pedal with some of these strategies. I never crate my dogs when I go out these days due to separation anxiety. However, I always crate one of my dogs, Sammie, when I leave due to living next door to the Ministry of Defense, where lots of bangs go off randomly. Loud bangs tend to stress Sammie out when nobody is around, but when she is in her crate, she feels safe and secure and sleeps. I know that if they suffered separation anxiety, these are the tools I would bring into play to help ease the worry and stress they are experiencing.

CHAPTER 8

Adolescence: A New Type of Terror!

Now, guys—are you ready for this? Yes, I'm talking about your puppy's adolescence. The equivalent of their terrible teens. It's different for every puppy and will depend largely on their breed and size, but generally speaking, you're going to start experiencing a new type of terror somewhere around five to six months!

Now, I don't want to scare you—please be reassured that if you have been putting all your training into practice, this challenging period of your puppy's development will be a little bit easier.

Adolescence—in a dog?

Yes, just like humans, canines experience a period of adolescence during which they lose their babyish cuteness and begin to morph into the adult dog you'll be spending the next ten to fifteen years with. Every dog goes through it, no exceptions, although some experience it more intensely than others. During your puppy's adolescence, you'll see them start to push their own boundaries (and your buttons) as their confidence grows and they begin to explore the world around them and use their growing body, super senses, incredible strength, and coordination.

While it's often a very exciting period for a puppy, it's less thrilling for owners, who can feel like they have lost their puppy during this time and begin to wonder what has happened to all the training they have been working hard on. Adolescent puppies can be impulsive and bold and often seem to forget all of the obedience commands and other good behaviors that they have been taught.

I'm not going to sugarcoat it, it can be a tough, make-or-break period for many owners, and people begin to wonder if they have made a huge mistake getting a puppy. For this reason, it's not, as you might expect, the January after Christmas that people take their puppies to rescue centers, but later in the year, when their puppy hits six months old. This is often the time that people decide they can't keep their dogs because they feel they cannot cope with the willful and defiant creature who is now living in their house.

The good news is that adolescence doesn't last forever, usually between six months and a year. And if you can get some of the most difficult behaviors in check, it can also be a fascinating period, as you begin to see your dog's true personality emerge. So, if you are reading this while also pulling all your hair out and wondering how the hell you are going to cope with the adolescent puppy that is terrorizing your home, do not fear. This next bit is going to help you.

Welcome to your new dog

Adolescence is when you will see your dog's true personality arrive, and you will start to see all of their breed-specific traits begin to kick in. If you've got a spaniel, maybe you'll start to notice them beginning to enjoy games of fetch. If you've got a sighthound, perhaps you'll begin to see their incredible speed start to build up on walks, terriers will enjoy ragging with tug toys, and so on.

This is when the breed fulfillment I told you about in chapter 1 begins to become so important. You need to play to your puppy's strengths. If you don't, that's when things start to go wrong. The first and most important thing you can do with your adolescent puppy is understand their breed requirements and ensure they are being met. A greyhound who doesn't get to run is going to flip out. A collie whose incredible brainpower is understimulated will make your life hell. Revisit your breed knowledge and ensure you are doing everything possible to meet your puppy's innate needs.

It's also important at this time to make sure you are reinforcing positive messaging with your puppy. It is very tempting to shout and generally lose your sh*t with a dog who has just eaten your new sofa, but that's not going to get you or your puppy anywhere. They'll just hear anger and noise and you'll be stressed. It's a pointless exercise all around, folks.

When dealing with a boisterous and disobedient adolescent, the best thing you can do is take your training back to basics.

Why? Because you want your dog to feel good about themselves, like they are doing something right, because doing the right thing gets them the treats and the fuss. Even though you might think you've got SIT sorted out and you're really bored with going over the same old commands repeatedly, I want you to do exactly that. Revisit your basic commands and use your marker words, do anything that is an easy win for your dog and an easy win for you. SIT, reward. SIT, reward. When you are in the midst of a tricky adolescent period, this is the best way to reassure yourself and your puppy that you have got this. Your puppy will calm down, and your mental health will be restored.

Leash walking and introducing HEEL

I am revisiting leash walking in detail right now because it is the key to having a well-behaved dog. Ensuring you have decent leash work during this adolescent period will help reduce so many unwanted behaviors. It helps you maintain your hard-won pecking order in the sense that your dog is following you daily, going where you go, stopping when you stop, and generally taking all their cues from you.

To be clear, leash walking is pretty much the most common problem I see with my clients, regardless of the type or size of dog they are walking. Once we successfully address leash walking, many other issues quickly disappear. Remember, guys, when you are walking your dog, you're also building a relationship. Even though you might think you're off to pick up the kids from nursery school, in your dog's mind, you are off on an adventure together . . . and you are the expedition leader!

Remember: Your dog hasn't forgotten everything you taught them, even if they behave like they have! Patience is key during adolescence, so be prepared to go over things and repeat things. It is worth doing this even if it does feel like everything is taking twice as long.

Danger: Do not let your puppy off the leash too soon. I've touched on this on page 34, but I just want to say it again, folks: Do not let your puppy run free off the leash before they are ready. This is a massively common mistake that can—and does—end in tragedy. Many people are lured into a false sense of security because of how well their puppy behaves during puppyhood. You should not even contemplate removing the leash while out in the park until they are at least 18 months old, once you have survived puppyhood and adolescence.

Heel time

By the time they reach adolescence, your puppy should be accustomed to walking on the leash without pulling. If you feel you need to revisit some of the basics, go back to pages 62–65 and double down on your leash walking practice. Even if you are now comfortably going for longer walks in different environments (socialization), you can still go back to basics, walking your puppy up and down your road or street just to reinforce everything they have learned so far.

As well as not massively pulling on the leash, your puppy should have a basic understanding of where the heel position is, even if you haven't actually been using the word. This is because you have been luring them to your side to reward them with a treat every time they stop pulling. So, in theory, your puppy already knows how to come to HEEL; you just haven't told them the name of this move yet!

Now, in adolescence, is a good time to start adding in that structure and direction of the HEEL command because it helps you stay in control and reminds your puppy that you're the source of all the good things in life.

Introducing new tools

Adolescence is a time for going over your basics, but it's also a time when you can start to introduce a few new, handy training tools to help with your puppy's development. Before I go into anything in detail, I just want to be clear: it is vitally important to remember that, whatever training tool you choose to implement, you must understand how to fit it correctly, how to teach your dog what it means, and how to use it safely. Without the proper use of these things, they can be detrimental and damaging to your pup's training.

Halti

If your adolescent puppy is still pulling on the leash despite all the basic leash walking training I've taken you through, you might choose to try a Halti leash. I'm a big fan of Haltis, as they make a massive difference with dogs who continue to have pulling problems, especially reactive dogs who can pull unexpectedly. A Halti is a gentle head harness that controls the dog by the snout and takes all the pressure off the throat.

To introduce a Halti, you must first make sure your puppy is comfortable putting their nose into the Halti. Do this by simply slipping it on and off and rewarding your puppy heavily for this (YES, and a treat). You'll then need to get your puppy comfortable with having the Halti done up, so again, go heavy on the rewards and praise. Then you need to master walking your puppy with a Halti on in a low-distraction environment (i.e., your garden or somewhere else familiar, without loads of other dogs and people). Once your dog is comfortable moving around your garden, you can move to outside; get your dog comfortable in your street before moving on to high-distraction-level areas, such as parks. A decent structured walk should be ten minutes, with your dog nicely walking by your side, followed by five minutes where you allow your puppy to sniff and explore a little, before returning to a more structured HEEL walk.

> **TIP:** *Haltis can be tricky to put on at first, so watch a few online videos or ask a friend to demonstrate theirs just to get a feel for how they work. Waving a Halti around and getting your puppy into a right old state about it before they've even tried walking with it will not help things go smoothly!*

Front clip harness with a double-ended leash

For mild pulling, and with puppies in general, a front clip harness used with a double-clipped leash on the collar (one end to the collar, one to the front clip harness) can be a great method to help reduce pulling. It will give you control of the head and body and make it much easier to steer/guide the dog to where you want them to be.

Final Thoughts

Adolescence is different for every dog; for some dogs, you would hardly even know they were in their teenage years, whereas others won't let you forget it. However, the real trick to surviving adolescence is getting those puppy foundations right and continuing to fortify them through the adolescent phase.

CHAPTER 9

Frequently Asked Questions

Guys, as you know, having a puppy comes with lots of questions. I've compiled a list of some of the most commonly asked questions I get every day from puppy owners.

Is it OK for puppies to be on the sofa?

Yes, it's absolutely fine for puppies to be on the sofa—once they have learned to settle down in the crate. When they are going in their crate with next to no protest and it has become their place of relaxation, you can start to introduce dog beds and the sofa, should you wish to. If you don't want a dog on your sofa, just don't put them on the sofa!

What to do if the puppy has a toilet accident

The reality is, you don't do anything other than clean it up! It was actually your fault for not paying attention to the signs that your dog needed to go to the toilet. Having a regular puppy routine helps reduce the chances of accidents. Under any circumstances, DO NOT RUB YOUR DOG'S NOSE IN THEIR OWN POO! This will only traumatize your puppy and may even make them afraid to go to the toilet in your presence . . . yes, even in your garden if you are present. This method is outdated and archaic. Your puppy will need to go to the toilet when they first wake up and before they go back down for a nap. Look for the signs. Your dog's nose glued to the floor, moving back and forth erratically, could be a sign that your dog needs to go for a pee.

Why do we have to have a leash inside the house?

Puppies are very much like toddlers; they will get into everything in a heartbeat. The leash helps you maintain control, remove your dog from situations in a nonconfrontational manner, and will make your life easier.

When do I stop using the indoor leash?

There is no set age for this; every dog is different. The general rule is when you do not need to use it anymore—because the dog is listening to your voice commands, behaving in the house, and knows how to switch off.

What should I do if my puppy is chewing their leash?

I find that the quickest way to stop leash chewing is this: when it is in the puppy's mouth, very firmly give a sharp tug on the leash. Do this quickly without emotion as if you are ripping off a Band-Aid and the puppy should soon stop chewing the leash.

How to stop your puppy from stealing things

Similar to your puppy having an accident, if your pup steals things, it is largely down to your leaving things around for them to pick up! Puppies will literally pick up anything that is new and out of the ordinary, or easily accessible, so in the beginning stages of training, don't leave tempting things lying around that your pup can easily get. Remember, puppies sample the world with their mouths. When a puppy is awake, this is the time you should be interacting with the puppy and training. If you can't because you are occupied elsewhere, they should be in a puppy pen with something to keep them occupied, like a KONG or brain puzzle.

What is the difference between a puppy pen and a crate, and why do I need both?

A crate is basically your dog's bedroom; it's where they go to sleep and learn to switch off—it becomes their safe space, a den-like environment. Your pup should go into their crate after regular training sessions to help achieve this, and the crate door must always be shut once you place them in the crate. A puppy pen is a place you can safely leave your puppy when you are busy and have not had time to get that energy out of the puppy—like a child's playpen. It's a secure enclosure that you put the pup in with their favorite toys to keep them occupied.

What do I do if my puppy cries when I leave the room?

If you have just put them down for a nap in their crate, then don't panic; it's completely normal. However, if the puppy is full of beans and has already had a nap, you can use your puppy pen and give them a little chew to keep them occupied as, sometimes, we have to leave the room. This creates a positive association with you leaving and coming back. This will also reduce the chances of them crying when you leave the room.

I found a puppy tooth; what do I do?

You may find the odd puppy "milk tooth" here and there; that's completely normal and nothing to worry about. The reality is that you will never find most of their teeth as they swallow them while they are eating.

Will I still form a good bond with my dog if I don't hand-feed?

Although for me hand-feeding is an absolute game changer and will speed up your training, there are other factors such as breed fulfillment, consistency with training, keeping your pup safe during stressful situations, and adequate mental and physical exercise that also contribute massively to a strong bond with your pup.

What are the best dog treats to use if you are not hand-feeding?

My top three go-to treats are: JR Pet Products' paté, tripe sticks (break these into small pieces), and liver cake.

At what age can I start to leave my puppy home alone?

Your puppy can be left home alone from day one, but it's important to remember that your puppy must always be safe and secure when they are left and cannot be left for longer than they can hold their bladder.

How long can I leave my puppy in their crate?

Never more than an hour or two at the beginning, but this is not set in stone. Your puppy will obviously be in the crate longer overnight than it is during the day, although even at night, I think no longer than four hours at any one time. However, once your pup has full bladder control, it will be fine in the crate overnight.

Is doggy day care a good idea?

It depends. A lot of doggy day-care centers are run like Disneyland for dogs. There is very little structure; all the dogs do is play, play, and play. This can become very problematic and undo the obedience and structure you have been teaching them. I don't usually recommend doggy day care to my clients. However, if you are going to send your dog to one, then make sure it is run by a dog trainer who teaches proper socializing, including teaching dogs to coexist in a calm, neutral, relaxed way around other dogs. A dog walker is a good alternative if you need someone to check in on your puppy and break up the day for them while you are working. A decent dog walker should discuss and follow your training regimen.

My puppy has suddenly gone off training; what should I do?

Dog training can feel like an endless pursuit of perfection, and sometimes when we are pushing a dog to improve, we can forget the importance of just having fun! Remember, all work and no play is no fun for anyone. If your pup has gone off training, go back a step or two, do something easy that your pup knows well, and give them frequent wins.

CONCLUSION

Hopefully, you have made it to the end of this book in one piece. You should have a much better understanding of what it takes to raise the perfect puppy. But I just want you to know that if you feel you are struggling and you are having bad days, that is frikkin' normal! It will get easier; I promise you that.

The whole purpose of this book is to guide you through puppyhood and to help you teach your puppy how to behave properly in human society as they grow up. This book is about getting your foundations right and surviving that difficult stage of adolescence so that you can spend the next ten years going anywhere with your dog.

And remember, you are going to have your dog for the next ten to fifteen years! Being strict now, following the instructions in this book, practicing your puppy routine daily for the first year of your dog's life will make all the years to come so much easier and enjoyable. Dogs don't live nearly long enough, in my opinion. So you need to make the most of it! You can either spend the first year being a bit strict and getting it right, or the rest of the dog's life stressing about not being able to do the things you want because you put cuddles ahead of training.

A well-trained dog is a joy to have in your life, but they do not get there overnight. You will cry, the dog will cry, but when you get there, you'll realize that everything was worth it. I lost Daisy in December 2019. I take comfort in the fact that I always did what was best for her and set aside my needs for her needs. We enjoyed adventure after adventure together and traveled the country helping thousands of dogs with their issues. For the last ten years, I have devoted my life to helping dogs and people. I live for this sh*t!

Dog training is an endless pursuit of perfection. It's not always going to be sunshine and rainbows, but that's all part of the fun. If you follow the advice in this book, you can also raise the perfect family dog that we all hope for when we set off on our puppy journey. And remember, you always have the Southend Dog Training community to help you every step of the way.

See you later, guys!
Adam

www.southenddogtraining.co.uk
Southend Dog Grooming
Southend Dog Nutrition

ABOUT THE AUTHOR

Adam Spivey began training dogs in 2012 and very quickly built up an amazing reputation. His straight-talking approach to training and no nonsense attitude have won him legions of fans and clients.

In December 2019, Adam met Evan (actually, Evan called on Adam to help him with his dog) and one thing led to another. Between them they decided to partner up and develop an online training platform, with more than 3.5 million followers and 12,000 members worldwide.